WEALTH & TAXABLE CAPACITY

WEALTH
AND TAXABLE CAPACITY

THE
NEWMARCH LECTURES FOR 1920-1
ON CURRENT STATISTICAL PROBLEMS
IN WEALTH AND INDUSTRY

BY

SIR JOSIAH STAMP

BOOKS FOR LIBRARIES PRESS
FREEPORT, NEW YORK

HJ2619
S7

First Published 1922
Reprinted 1971

INTERNATIONAL STANDARD BOOK NUMBER:
0-8369-5713-X

LIBRARY OF CONGRESS CATALOG CARD NUMBER:
79-150200

PRINTED IN THE UNITED STATES OF AMERICA

PREFACE.

THE Newmarch Lectures for 1920-1 were given at University College in February, 1921, upon "Current Statistical Problems in Wealth and Industry." They received a publicity in the Press that led to numerous requests for full publication, and I feared from this widespread interest that there might have been some misapprehension on the part of the public as to the character and purpose of the lectures. They were intended to be a detached examination of the chief statistical data available in the consideration of problems of wealth and industry, and an exposition of some principles involved in arriving at those details.

Newspaper readers seemed to scent a new supply of powder and shot for current social polemics. In this respect many may have been disappointed. It is with some misgivings that the lectures are now given the permanence of book form, for while the principles have, so to speak, some enduring quality, and it is urgent that they should be better understood, the grounds for more popular interest seem to lie in the illustrations of those principles expressed in current values, which are necessarily quite ephemeral.

At a time when the national income is probably decreasing every month (in its monetary expression) at the rate of 100 million £ per annum, any illustra-

PREFACE

tion based on current values is out of date before the printer's ink is dry, and indeed, however correct it may have been as a rate at a given moment of time, it may never have been correct at all over a *period* of time to which it relates. It might have been better, therefore, if the illustrative figures could have been drawn from a period of more stable values. The risk of being quoted without context or reservations has, however, been faced, and readers are asked, upon the early arrival of a time when some of the estimates must be manifestly inapplicable to changed conditions, and have no lasting value, to bear these reservations in mind. It may well be some years before a condition of stable values is reached. There is much, therefore, to be said, if such considerations as these are to be published at all, against holding them back until more permanent illustrations of principle can be given.

This attempt to outline some of the elementary principles involved in the valuation of National capital and income and the determination of their distribution and their relation to prices, taxation and public debt, necessarily suffers from the defects of lecture form. It is, therefore, with much diffidence and a sense of their shortcomings that the lectures are now embodied in book form.

So far as the field of wages is concerned, it is pre-eminently Dr. Bowley's own, and I here acknowledge my full obligations to him for my numerous citations from his work.

J.C.S.

December, 1921.

CONTENTS

CHAPTER I.

THE MEASUREMENT OF NATIONAL CAPITAL

(1) *Introduction: Essential Data to be considered.*

ANY student of current financial and commercial problems will realise that in the discussion of them there are certain boundaries or limits which condition the possible treatment of the subject. We have been, for example, recently made familiar with the idea that there is a limit to taxable capacity. These points represent, so to speak, physical facts which we may deplore but cannot escape, and all our political strategy and economic practice has to be conformed to them just as military or other action must be limited by geography and topography.

Now, although these facts exist, our precise measurement of them is often very faulty, and what is more important still, our appreciation of the exact meaning of our measurements when we have made them, is also very slipshod ; we ignore real differences of meaning and apply various unlike things to the same problem as

2 WEALTH & TAXABLE CAPACITY

though we had already carefully defined them. These essential data of modern discussions include the amount of the national wealth. This, in itself, covers three or four distinct ideas, such as the amount of taxable wealth in the hands of, first, individuals and collections of individuals, or, secondly, the State, and, thirdly, the amount that would fall under particular schemes of taxation, "chopping" off sections of wealth at a particular moment of time; while there are such other concepts as "inventory wealth" and "living capital" which have a use for particular purposes. Then we have the national income, which also is capable of several distinct conceptions, and may, or may not, include those classes of income which are not the subject of money payments, or which are not customarily treated as income. Then follows the way in which the above-mentioned wealth or income is divided up amongst individuals ; that is, the proportion of it which goes to certain sections of our population ; the amount of income which is not consumed but is saved ; the amount of it which is made at home, and that which arises from abroad ; the division of wealth into different categories of ownership, such as the owners of capital, the owners of muscle, and the owners of brain. Then we have the facts about these proportions or measurements, not merely as static problems at a particular moment of time, but such dynamic problems as the *rate* at which they may be altering, and the direction of any change.

Further determinable points are now to be found in the requirements of the State for purposes of the National Debt, and, perhaps, also in the amount of individual income or wealth which is available for State purposes without reducing the individual to a state of starvation or of universal ca' canny—in other words, what we now call " the limit of taxab!e capacity." Other limits of an inexorable character are to be found in the effect of changes of price upon incomes and wealth in relation to tax burdens.

(2) *The Spirit and Purpose of the Enquiry.*

Now people would very much rather discuss principles and propaganda, and proposed tactics for social legislation, than do the trying work of examining the statistical data upon which nearly all such discussions are based. These data are tossed about as things given, requiring no further examination, or of which the examination is complete ; whereas until we have thoroughly examined them and know the limits of error in amount to which they may be subject, and their precise character for any particular problem, we are hardly entitled to embark upon the discussion at all.

I have been impressed with the great necessity
for a better public recognition of the methods
and principles involved in getting at these
essential data, and of what they really mean.
I am, therefore, frankly devoting these lectures
to such an examination, and if I may so call it,
a popularisation of the purely statistical investigations involved. I think it, for example,
highly important that there should be a wider
knowledge of the various ways in which the
national wealth can be computed—the limits
of error, the uses to which the valuations may
be put, and the modifications required, according to the several uses to which they are devoted.
I think it essential that we should have a better
knowledge of the unescapeable facts about the
division of income, and the amounts available
for particular purposes. If, therefore, I do not
attempt solutions for our great public problems to-day, and you are inclined to accuse me
of not being practical on that account, my answer
would be that I am trying to be practical in a
higher sense, in that I want to understand the
real limits to knowledge and discussion, which
are a preliminary to these things. As Professor
Pigou says in his great book recently published,
" When a man sets out upon any course of
enquiry the object of his search may be either
light or fruit, either knowledge for its own sake,
or knowledge for the sake of the good things
to which it leads." I do not pretend that the

facts which we are proposing to examine have any interest apart from their application, but it is a feature of prime scientific importance that we should examine them in the dry light of statistical precision before we proceed to cloud our judgment by application to specific problems in which, try as we will, we must be influenced by prepossession and prejudice. We should be like the man who would not admit that two plus two made four until he was told what use was going to be made of the admission. The statistician who begins with his thesis for social betterment, and then produces his figures to support it, may be perfectly honest, but he is always under the suspicion of having been unduly influenced by the goal at which he is aiming.

(3) *The National Wealth—the Questions to be Answered.*

The first cardinal feature for determination is the National Wealth :

(1) What is its amount and to what degree of accuracy ?   (2) How is it computed ? (3) What does the result mean when we have got it ?   (4) What precautions have we to take in applying it ?   (5) Are there different figures for different applications or purposes? (6) What are those purposes ?

While there is a very considerable literature upon this particular subject—running into some scores of works—it is extraordinary how the less responsible efforts, often mere partisan guesses, gain a footing and keep currency with serious and reasoned estimates. This arises partly from the fact that the partisan who is out to prove his point is nearly always best pleased by an extreme figure, and so we find that current estimates of the wealth of the United Kingdom (in 1914) used in polemical literature range from 10,000 millions to 24,000 £ sterling.

(4) *The Use of such Estimates.*

The uses to which Estimates of National Wealth and Income may be put are many and various. They include:—

(1) Tests of "progress" by way of comparisons between different years, to show the accumulation of capital ; tests of the distribution of wealth, according to the form or embodiment which wealth takes ; of the effects of changes in the rate of interest, or in the value of money.

(2) Tests of the relative "prosperity" or resources of different nations or communities, either as a whole or per head of the population, and in relation to their national debts.

(3) Comparisons of income with capital and property.

(4) Considerations of the distribution of wealth according to individual fortunes, and changes in that distribution.

(5) Consideration of the applicability and yield of schemes of taxation, *e.g.*, the capital levy.

(6) Questions relating to War indemnities.

It is in connection rather with the second, fifth and sixth classes above that the public mind is most exercised at the present moment, and a great deal of careful, as well as careless, work has quite recently been done in this field of statistics.*

It is, perhaps, hardly necessary to say that the capital wealth or incomes *at any given moment* is not a sole test of ability to bear indemnities—it is only a. partial measure, for the potential wealth in ungotten minerals and resources, as well as the character of commerce and *distribution* of income, are important factors in the problem. It may, however, be pointed out at once that present values are on a very different scale from those which are being discussed, and the true money measure of present wealth can only be guessed at for some time yet.

As I shall show presently, still the best, and, indeed, the only way, to estimate present wealth is to start with the pre-war figures and make what modifications and adjustments the changed circumstances indicate as desirable. Moreover, the pre-war figure is in itself full of importance for comparison and general interest.

(5) *What is meant by National Wealth?*

The wealth of a country may mean *either* the value of the objects found within its boundaries, *or* the wealth of the inhabitants, including their

* Vide *Statistical Journal*, May, 1919.

foreign possessions, and excluding wealth within the country held by people abroad. The confusion between these two ideas has played havoc with discussions on such subjects as the "Taxable Capacity of Ireland." It is the latter sense—the wealth of the inhabitants—that is mainly under consideration. That aspect is foremost when questions of taxation are prominent, but there are matters, such as the inalienable wealth of a country in a geographical sense (for warlike purposes) for which the former is important. A colony capitalised from the home country may be poor judged by the wealth of its inhabitants, but rich in its resources and the actual yield within its borders.

(6) *Kinds of Ownership*.

Wealth in private hands is not easy to define exactly, for there are various shades of ownership :

(a) Absolute personal disposition of the whole value.

(b) Trust interests.

(c) Collective ownership with only potential specific allocation to individuals, such as the reserves of a company, which may be of higher value than the aggregation of the market value of individual interests therein (as tested by the Stock Exchange difference in prices of the shares with, and without, such reserves.)

(d) Collective ownership, without the possibility of individual allocation, social private wealth, such as churches, clubs, etc.

Similarly, communal wealth is not all of the same degree of " dispersion " in value.

(a) City and local property like waterworks, buildings and trams, having a " value " determinable by deliberate comparison with privately owned objects.

(b) National property, varying from a museum to a navy.

The closeness with which a " market value " can be assigned varies with the class of wealth for, if there is no possibility of a market, one naturally tends towards the adoption of the cost of production or reproduction. Moreover, some of the comparisons of national wealth of different countries are slightly impaired by the extent to which the methods employed give different recognition of each class.

Until recent questions of taxable capacity, and the yield of capital levies arose, we understood national wealth to mean the full wealth of our inhabitants, derived from sources at home and abroad, and also the amount of capital here owned by people abroad, which was not striking, so that earlier writers never troubled much to exclude it.

(7) *Methods of Computing Wealth.*

There are five distinct methods of computing national wealth in vogue, but different countries do not rely on them equally, nor are they always able to employ them all.

They are :

(1) Based on data arising through taxation of income —notably the United Kingdom.

(2) Based on data arising through the annual taxation of Capital—notably United States.

(3) Based on data arising through taxation of Capital at irregular periods–Death Duties.–Notably Italy and France.

(4) The inventory—an aggregation of various forms of wealth built up from various sources, insurance, etc. —Notably France and Germany.

(5) The Census.—Notably Australia.

We rely chiefly upon the first, but we fortify it considerably by the third, and check large sections of it by the fourth.

(8) *Recent Estimates.*

The most recent detailed estimates of capital are those given by Mr. Crammond before the Royal Statistical Society in 1914, £16,472,000, before the Royal Statistical Society in 1914 £16,472,000,000, and my own in "British Incomes and Property" (published in 1916), for 1914, of £14,319,000,000±£1,867,000,000. The latter was re-examined in 1918 in the " Economic Journal," in connection with the proposals for a capital levy which had brought forth a crop of " estimates " widely divergent. The former was repeated by Mr. Crammond recently without re-examination.

The estimates by Sir Bernard Mallet and Mr. Strutt given to the Statistical Society in 1915, based on the "multiplier," led apparently to a considerably lower figure than my estimate, but the difference has now been fairly reconciled.*

* *Economic Journal,* 1918.

At the risk of wearying you, I propose to take you, in some little detail, through the main workings for the estimate, briefly indicating the kind of checks upon it, by going over Mr. Crammond's and my own side by side. This will serve two purposes. First, I have undertaken to give you some idea how these things are worked. Secondly, I wish to make the statement once again that Mr. Crammond's estimate contains demonstrable errors in its make up and does not " fit " with the main auxiliary checks we possess.

In passing, we shall get a glimpse of some of the chief statistical difficulties confronting us.

(9) *Estimates by the Capitalisation Method.*

The Income Tax provides us with some first-hand statistics of values and profits in useful categories, much more useful for our purpose than merely knowing the number of people with incomes of certain amounts. The statistics for each class were given until recent years in the annual reports of the Commissioners of Inland Revenue.

The following table sets out the details of the two Estimates side by side, and also the extent to which Mr. Crammond's figures exceed my own :

£'000 *omitted.*

	E.C.	J.C.S.	Deviations.	
			+	—
Sch. A.				
Lands	1,305	1,155	150	–
Houses	3,357	3,330	27	–
Other Profits ...	32	22	10	–
Sch. B.				
Farmers' Profits ..	140	340	–	200
Sch. C.				
Public funds, less				
Home Funds.				
Government and				
Local Property ...	1,451	1,548	–	97
Sch. D.				
Quarries, Mines				
and Ironworks	92	216	–	124
Gasworks, Water-				
works, Canals,				
Docks fishing,				
etc.	444	460	–	16
Railways	1,152	1,143	9	–
Railways out of				
the U.K. ...	560	655	–	95
Foreign & Colonial				
Securities and				
Coupons... ...	1,017	1,004	13	–
Other Profits and				
Interest ...	233	276	–	43
	9,783	10,149	209	575
Trades and busi-				
nesses including				
for income evad-				
ing assessment ..	3,789	2,770	1,019	–
Income accruing				
abroad and not				
remitted ..	900	400	500	–
Income of non-tax				
paying classes				
derived from				
capital	1,000	200	800	–
Furniture, etc. ..	1,000	800	200	–
	16,472	14,319	2,728	575

+2,153

(a) Classified Sources of Income.

Mr. Crammond took 25 years' purchase of the gross Sch. A. Assessment on Lands, whereas it was demonstrable that the average value was not more than 21 years' purchase, although 25 years was possibly applicable to the net assessment.

He had not taken sufficient notice of the change in the rate of interest since Giffen's time, of the actual sales taking place in the market, and of the average valuations adopted for Estate Duty purposes for rented property. From the resultant difference of about 210 millions, I allowed for certain special features in Scotland and for an under assessment in Ireland, and for the special value of building lands, serving to reduce the difference—which became 150 millions.

In the case of houses and premises generally, Mr. Crammond took 15 years for the gross assessment. I took 14 years for the gross assessment, after making certain adjustments, and 17.4 upon the net, adopting the mean result.

The difference for the year taken by Mr. Crammond would have been over 200 millions between us, but as I worked upon a later year with an additional rental of 9 million £ it was greatly reduced, and stands at 27 million £ only.

In the small item of other profits, I made a
careful analysis of the nature of the income and
adopted 21 years, whereas Mr. Crammond kept
to an old precedent with 25 years.

In the case of farmers, Mr. Crammond adopted
the Sch. B. assessment at 8 years' purchase, but
as this assessment was notoriously below the
profits being made at the time (being just prior
to the date when the basis was altered from
one-third to the full rent, as the rough equivalent
of profits), I preferred to ignore the altogether
useless tax figures, and to review the various
estimates of agricultural capital made by
agricultural writers, and the accumulation of
evidence before the Royal Commission on agriculture, checked by more recent ideas as to
the average amount per acre. In taking 340
million against his 140 million, I added 200
millions to his figures.

In dealing with Schedule C. or the interest
upon Government Stocks, Mr. Crammond followed Giffen's method by deducting the
Consols, and so not allowing the amount of
the national debt to swell the total of the
national wealth. I followed a course which
comes to the same net result, viz., capitalising
the whole interest which is the wealth of individuals, but deducting the amount of the
National Debt from the value of Government
and local property. The gross amount of this
property I put at about 1,100 millions against

Mr. Crammond's 750 millions, but taking the two items together, I have only 97 millions in excess of his figures. In getting the value for Government and local property, I reduced the figures taken by Giffen, Money and others, by eliminating what had been included twice over by previous writers, viz., the value of waterworks, gasworks, trams, etc., the profits of which as trading undertakings are included in the other classified statements of profit for taxation purposes.

Mr. Crammond's estimate was $92\frac{1}{2}$ millions for quarries, mines and ironworks, whereas I gave 179 for mines only and 37 for ironworks, so that I exceeded him by 124 millions. A glance at the evidence given before the Coal Commission and the details of balance sheets and Excess Profits Duty capital show that my figures were very closely justified. Mr. Crammond's are demonstrably too low, upon a tonnage basis. The difference is due partly to the fact that the profits of the years taken by him were rather lower, but mainly to the fact that he took 4 years' purchase, and I adopted $9\frac{1}{2}$ years after closer enquiry.

In the case of Gasworks, Waterworks, Canals, Docks, fishings, etc., and railways, the difference is due solely to the difference of years.

For other profits and interest, and for foreign securities, I made a somewhat closer examination, and there are slight differences in the multipliers adopted, but the net alteration is quite small.

(b) General Business Profits.

My total estimate up to this point exceeds Mr. Crammond's by 366 million £, and it is at this stage they diverge more seriously. Mr. Crammond adheres to Giffen's old classification, " Other public companies " which he takes at 15 years' purchase, and " trades and professions " which are also taken at 15 years, treating one-fifth of the profits as capable of capitalisation. To the profits of trades and professions, he adds one-fifth for omission or evasion. His resultant total for businesses is, therefore, 3,787 millions.

Sir Leo Chiozza-Money's method in " Riches and Poverty " was to take the *whole* class of profits " Businesses otherwise detailed," and to treat one-half as capable of capitalisation at 10 per cent. For the year 1912 taken on Mr. Crammond's estimate, Money's method would give 2,109 millions, a difference of 1,679 millions. If the companies formed half of the whole trade profits, Crammond's method would be equal to the average of 3 and 15 years' purchase or 9 years over all—as a matter of fact, as the companies are a growing proportion, the actual rate adopted is higher. Money's is equivalent to 5 years' purchase over all. The matter is so important that those interested should read the substance of my own enquiry into it, showing the reason why I adopted an inter-mediate course.* It is quite clear from an examination of ordinary stock investment values in the years 1911 to 1913, that the average company business was not worth more than 11 years' purchase of net profits.

I first purged the assessment total of its overcharges and reductions, the inclusion of salaries and especially the allowance for " wear and tear." The latter was generally alleged to be insufficient, and therefore, if anything, my capitalisation would on that account be too high. But no effort had been made by others to get a proper basis figure upon which to work. I then added for evasion 17 millions in place of Mr. Crammond's quite excessive item of 44½ millions. The mean of the two methods gave me 2,770 millions or just over 1,000 millions less than Mr. Crammond's estimate. It must not be forgotten in comparing the number of years' purchase adopted in capitalising profits assessed to Income Tax Schedule D with the rate of interest on Stock Exchange investments, that the most secure part of the profits, that repre-sented by real property, owned and occupied for business, has been deducted and assessed

* *British Incomes and Property.* Chapter XI. (a) There was a great change in the character of Company profits between 1895 and 1914. (b) Registration as joint stock companies gave profits an unreal status in capitalisation compared with private ownership.

under Sch. A and the number of years' purchase applicable to the remainder is therefore lower than it would otherwise be, whereas the profit known to the Stock Exchange, except where there were debentures, includes this stabler element. The record of " paid up " Capital of Companies, some 2,700 millions, is, of course, little test of the true market value that we are seeking. We have to deduct the companies in liquidation, and a very large sum for duplication of capital by interholdings, then the value of real property owned, and also all the colliery and other companies that have been dealt with elsewhere separately. Again, much share capital covers holdings in Consols and foreign securities, also separately capitalised. The total share capital comparable with the figures we are considering is therefore quite indeterminate, but it is very much less, and then we must add, per contra, the declared or secret reserves, and deduct a sum for share capital which covers goodwill no longer existent. The statistics of share capital clearly cannot be brought in aid to confirm or refute the estimates. I have shown that the method of the Census of Production in estimating the capital in manufacturing industries covered by the Census, gave results which agree closely with those yielded by my method of capitalising the profits.*

* Vide *Economic Journal*, 1918. Also Professor Bowley's *Division of the Product of Industry*.

There are no other subsidiary checks for this section taken by itself, except the results of business valuations for the purpose of Estate Duty. Those who incline to put a high multiplier to the total figures of assessed profits must remember that over the large field of the smaller businesses, the bulk of the profit represents earnings of management, which are personal and not readily capitalised, while only a small part is interest on capital.

Moreover, a certain amount of trading loss may not be reflected in the figures, while the profits make no allowance for " wasting asset " elements.

Mr. Crammond has an item of 44½ millions of income for trades and professions evading income tax, which was pure guess work based on the ideas of thirty years previously, when evasion was a very different matter from what it became in 1914. My figure to correspond was a closely and anxiously examined one, viz., 17 million £. Mr. Crammond's capitalisation gave 133 million £ on this account, and the total difference between us for the capitalisation of business profits is 1,222 million £.

The next item is the capital belonging to non-income tax paying classes, which he puts at 1,000 millions against my 200 millions, because he had wrongly supposed that, being exempt from income tax, nothing was included on that account in the Income Tax Statistics. My comment in "British Incomes and Property" was as follows :—

"It must be clearly understood that this item does not really refer to the *savings* of the exempt classes. These savings are in savings banks, and provident societies, all of which make investments, or in building societies which have a gross income from real property, and there is hardly any channel of savings which has not been fully represented in the *gross* income tax assessments already capitalised. Sixty millions of exempt income has already been accounted for at various rates, from fifteen years' purchase upwards, or, say, over 1,000 millions. What remains is the capital value of the stock in trade, implements, and utensils, etc., of small shop-keepers, and workers like blacksmiths, etc. Anyone familiar with the prices at which small businesses are taken over will hardly quarrel with an *average* capital of £200 for the shops and £100 for workshops. If we take the table on page 63 of the "Statistical Journal," 1910, giving the British Association Committee's estimate of the amount and distribution of income (other than wages) below the exemption limit, we shall find that working capital of this description is confined mainly to classes 25 to 28, 30 and 31. On the most liberal estimate of average capital for the numbers given there, it is difficult to account

for more than £200,000,000. Approaching the
matter in another way, we have in England and
Wales about 534,000 shops and licensed houses,
of which, speaking generally, those over £40
only will contain income tax payers, leaving
370,000 under £40. Adding for Scotland and
Ireland, we may thus account for £80,000,000.
Then 400,000 cases of workshops, etc., at an
average of £100 and a million workers with
tools, etc., of an average value of £10, bring the
total to £130,000,000. There may also be some
forms of investment which escape the gross
income tax assessment, but, altogether,
£200,000,000 is a sufficient estimate."

Under the heading " movable property," etc.,
not yielding income (furniture, etc.), he has
1,000 million £ against my figure of 800
million £. This is admittedly most difficult,
but everyone who has examined the matter
critically, in the light of Estate Duty valuations
(which would not have given a higher figure
than 200 millions), and what is common knowledge as to the general ratio of furniture values
to rental values, gives results of the lower order.
Finally, under the heading of Income from
Investments Abroad or from shipping banking
and mercantile services not brought home,
Mr. Crammond puts £60,000,000, which he
capitalises at 15 years, giving a capital of 900
million £. My estimate was 400 million £ as
at that date. He followed Giffen's earlier

C

work, and as that was full of misconceptions as to the nature of the Income Tax figures, which I have fully shown in " British Incomes," he naturally repeated the error. Hardly any writers have dealt with these foreign income figures without falling into serious technical error. My estimate of 20 millions income was supported by the Chancellor of the Exchequer's estimate of the duty to be derived from the alteration in law which made such income liable to tax, and nothing that has taken place since has shown it to be inadequate. Moreover, if this figure is included with the foreign income shown, the capitalisation I give accords better with the capital abroad independently ascertained by Sir George Paish than any other.

Under these last four headings my valuation is 4,170 million £, against Mr. Crammond's 6,689 million £,—a difference of 2,519 million £.

Unnecessary Conflicts of Statement lead to Confusion.

Mr. Crammond's estimate was originally given with practically no supporting evidence, or reasoned discussion, and some of his errors were pointed out at the time by me. He acknowledged the criticism as very valuable, and said he was " glad to accept the corrections." As Sir Alfred Soward and Mr. Willan say in their recent book, " Dr. Stamp adversely criticised the estimate, and the author seemingly did not defend it. Mr. Crammond, however, in 1918, reproduced his figure." It must be added that despite renewed criticism of it in May, 1919, before the Royal Statistical Society, when he was accused of not making himself sufficiently acquainted with the character of the original data, Mr. Crammond has continued to give his old estimate without any comment (beyond a disparagement of other estimates) unsupported by evidence. He repeated it in his address on British Finance Policy given to the Institute of Bankers, 28th June, 1921. This course, naturally, leads to confusion.

The most recent example that has come to my notice is Mr. Snowden's book "Labour and National Finance." When he comes to consider how much it would be possible to raise by means of a capital levy, he says " that estimates of the total capital vary very considerably." He refers to my estimate in September, 1918, of the pre-war amount that would have been available for a general levy—11,000 million £, amd my tentative estimate of the war increase of 5,250 million £, making 16,250 million £ available for a capital levy. He then says " Mr. Crammond, in a paper read before the Institute of Bankers, June 7th, 1920, estimated the national wealth at the present time as 24,000 million £. He arrived at this figure by taking his own estimate of the pre-war national wealth at 16,500 million £, which he said would represent, in post-war money, 27,500 million £. Mr. Crammond's figure agrees precisely with the estimate made by Mr. Sydney Arnold, namely, that for the purpose of the capital levy the taxable wealth of the country will amount to 24,000 million £. Mr. Pethick Lawrence has based his estimate of the yield of a capital levy on the assumption that the taxable capital of the country is about 15,000 million £. The wide disparity between the lower and higher of these various estimates is probably explained by the inclusion in Mr. Crammond's and Mr. Arnold's estimates of the war-loans as an addition to the capital of the country." " The war-loans," Mr. Snowden goes on to say, " do not represent any addition to the real capital, but it appears to be sound to regard these sums as available for the purpose of a capital levy." He then proceeds to accept Mr. Crammond's estimate and, with an average rate of tax of 14 per cent. to get 3,000 million £ as the yield of tax.

It need hardly be said that this loose way of handling the matter gets us no nearer to the real truth, and rather confuses the public. Although Mr. Snowden has had important details in front of him, he has not in any way grasped the immense difference between estimates of the National Wealth taken collectively, and an aggregation of individual fortunes, a difference which extends far beyond the question of the National Debt. The passage serves to show, moreover, that unsystematic and uncritical estimates such as those given by Mr. Crammond, may circulate, and be used on terms, equal—or often, indeed, superior—to estimates into which much careful thought and criticism has been put, and to which every known test has been applied. It is, first, totally wrong to imagine that the national wealth as a whole comes under any proposed levy, and, secondly, quite wrong to treat the War Loan as though it were wholly an addition to the wealth for this purpose. It is true that it is no addition at all to the *real* wealth of the country, but, on the other hand, it is equally true that only to a limited extent is it recognisable upon the wealth returns of individuals. The matter was very carefully gone into in the Board of Inland Revenue memorandum,* and it is surprising how small a section of this wealth can be regarded as " coming out " upon individual returns. Mr. Crammond's method of multiplying up an unchecked pre-war estimate by a general fall in currency values, with no reference whatever to the change in the actual market values of securities, and the rate of interest, is too loose and too rough to be treated seriously as a statistical estimate at all.

* *Vide* Report and Evidence : Select Committee on Increase of Wealth (War).

Against each detailed estimate I have given
a figure for the "range of doubt" which
expresses the limits within which the true
figure must certainly be found. Thus "gasworks 182 ±18" means that the value must
certainly lie between 164 and 200 million £.
Now, in my aggregate, I have given the aggregate range of error as 1,867 millions, which is
the figure that would result if all the detailed
estimates were wrong in the same direction
to the full extent. Everyone acquainted with
statistics or probabilities will know that this
is an extremely unlikely, indeed, almost impossible event, so that we may adopt a
common principle, and, after squaring each of
the details, take the square root of their
aggregate, which gives a range of possible error
of 860 millions. The *upper* limit of my estimate
is, therefore, 15,179 millions, and it can safely
be said that any pre-war estimate exceeding
15,000 millions will put its author into grave
difficulties, if he is to reconcile it with all the
existing data, and satisfy all possible tests.

Now, how this National valuation is con-
tradicted or confirmed by the other methods—
by what is known as the multiplier and the other
checks we have upon parts of it,—will be seen
to some extent later, when we have to bring
out some questions of distribution, which is
bound up with the points I have made already
as to the way in which property is owned.*

* *Vide* page 8

The Valuation To-day.

The next question is : How do we pass to the valuation at the present day ?

Apart from the difficult question of how property may be owned, we have three different possible conceptions of the valuation. First, we could arrive at the valuation to-day by taking the accepted valuation of some previous year as, for example, 1914, and adding to it the value of all additional physical wealth at its cost price, deducting, of course, any physical wealth that disappears or is destroyed, according to the figure at which it stood in our original valuation. This is the same thing as adding to the original valuation the amount of the capital savings out of current income, as the net amounts actually saved each year. This involves no reconsideration of original values in the light of changing money conditions, and cannot be treated as satisfactory for any ordinary purpose. Even before the recent great change in money values it was never the case that the difference between two valuations, say, ten or fifteen years apart, would equal the aggregate amount of net savings for the intervening years. That difference might be either more or less than the savings, according to the movement of money values, and the rate of interest. Thus it is dangerous to suppose that the valuation by Giffen of 10,037 millions in

1885, and that of 10,663 million £ in 1895, reflected an annual amount of saving of only 60 millions, the difference in ten years being 600 millions. The savings were offset by the changes in existing values, just as the whole current profits of a business might be used up if we made depreciation allowances for the changing value of its Balance Sheet assets brought about through the rate of interest.

Under a second method we might revalue all the physical assets as at a single moment of time. This is a little paradoxical, because all valuation involves the assessment of a flow of income over a period, and, therefore, valuation at a moment of time may seem to be a contradiction in terms. What is really involved is a question of degree leading into the third kind of valuation which, although ostensibly at a given moment of time, endeavours to take the more stable view, and to present a figure which would be approximately true if judged also at a single moment of time at some little distance. This point is of very material importance at a time like the present, with rapidly changing values. If we were to seize by an instantaneous photograph, the market prices of shares, etc., as at the 30th June, 1920, and to secure a similar picture to-day (Feb., 1921), we should see a very material difference, and we should have to make up our minds which is to be regarded as the estimate of national wealth for the year 1920.

Technical Difficulties in the Present Valuation.

There are special difficulties at the present time in the determination of the national capital—they are of two kinds : (1) in the material to be used ; and (2) in the principles involved.

Taking those affecting material :

First. The taxation data available have been reduced during the war, and some of the classifications previously useful have disappeared, at any rate, for a time.

Second. The statistics are always two years " behind," and in some senses five. Assessments themselves, for any given year, relate to the actual results of three preceding years (or five in some instances). So the assessment for the year ending 5th April, 1920, may be on the profits of the three years from 1st July, 1916, 1917, and 1918 respectively. These figures are the latest available, and they are, as may be seen, hardly emerging from purely war years, heavily charged with special war profits, and no use whatever as a basis for a firm capitalisation for the future.

Third. For some time to come the assessments to profits will still be reduced by the amount of Excess Profits Duty assessed. If these are really a burden upon profits, then, of course, it is only necessary to add the duty to get a result which represents profits without the duty, but if as so many urge, the burden is passed on, and profits are maintained, then removing the duty should have no effect on the profit. In the case of removal, it might have no effect upon the *rate* of profit, but might lead to wider trade and a large aggregate profit at the same *rate*. But with this burden about, as we think, to disappear, it would be bold to forecast the amount of future net profit which can form the basis of capitalisation.

Fourth. The assessed value of property is now on a valuation 10 years old, owing to the war having interfered with the regular reassessment. This may be remedied before very long. But, in any case, it relates to that field of the enquiry in which there is least uncertainty.

Fifth. The auxiliary tests are not available. We have had no Census of Production and no capital valuation of land for 10 years. The changes in the Death Duty Statistics are very slow in making themselves felt, or in giving such a basis of years that will warrant any close inferences. The multiplier depends upon mortality statistics which have been quite upset by the war.

Even such " inventory " methods as the capital *put into* businesses, mines, railways, etc., are of no value now, since the capital

sunk is no such criterion of future worth as it
may be when gold values have been relatively
stable for a long time.   Judging cotton mills
at " so much a spindle," and shipping at " so
much a ton," is a perilous proceeding when
such values are changing daily.

Difficulties in Principle.

*But more important still are the questions of
principle involved.*

The points of principle that arise at the
present time bring out various difficulties owing
to a temporary " hold up " in the normal flow of
economic forces.   Are we to value houses upon
their value as *investments* to the recipient of
rents, or upon the totally different figures which
we should get if we took the extraordinary
pressure of scarcity values created by an
enormous demand focussed upon a very small
point of effective supply ?   In the case of
commodities which, in the economic phrase,
have a " highly elastic demand," the change
in price is often out of all proportion to the
increase in demand.   A very few motor-cars
short of the requirements of the people who
are keen on cars, may serve to keep the price
very high.   On the whole, therefore, it would
appear advisable to ignore purely " scarcity "
values of things that are saleable commodities,

and to cling as closely as possible to investment values over a long period. But investment values in the case of houses are artificially low, because, even with a considerable supply, the cost of the production of houses is very much higher than of old, and rents left normally to themselves without legal restriction, would rise very much in the same ratio as other prices. Thus the capital value of such rents, even with the same multiplier or number of years' purchase, would be *pro tanto* higher. Of course the multiplier is actually less. Property generally forms so considerable a section of national wealth that the difference between these two views is material when we come to attack the figures.

Secondly, what I have said about valuation at a moment of time, may be illustrated by the very high prices of ships during the war. The profits to be derived from the ownership of a ship were so enormous for the immediate future that the capital value at any given moment represented not merely the anticipated average income over future years, but also the anticipation of a huge and abnormal sum to be received in the immediate future. Thus a ship fetching £400,000 might do so because it was anticipated that it would make £200,000 in the next twelve months whereas its normal value would have been £200,000 for an anticipated yield of anything from £15—£20,000 per annum. Now do we really intend to mix up what I call a " stable national capital " with a passing monetary receipt in the nature of income ?

Thirdly, take those classes of goods which provide an income of enjoyment or use rather than of money, such as jewellery and furniture, Are we to assess them at the present shop value of their equivalents, or to keep them at the figure that they originally cost us ? Here, again, an indeterminate and intermediate course seems to be the wiser for adoption to any one who is seeking some element of stability in his valuation. Furniture is essentially a thing which may rise to great heights of price through an immediate shortage of supply combined with a limited, but intense demand.

Fourthly, the valuation of businesses at a time when the future of taxation is so uncertain, and its burden so great, presents special points of difficulty. Is one to capitalise the present earnings accruing to the owner of the business, or the earnings which one imagines will accrue to him after the repeal of a special duty ?

Fifthly. It has been the practice to consider national property on conservative lines, viz., its estimated cost written down substantially for obsolescence and depreciation, but to-day we are faced with the fact that the cost of reproduction would be totally different.

You will see that apart from the question of temporary shortage, or a fluctuating point of monetary values, we are faced with the question of whether we shall go " the whole hog " in our revaluations, taking a new and assumed stable level of currency of an altogether different kind from that hitherto adopted. If we do not do this there is a mixture of different currency values, which is rather damaging to any inferences we may wish to draw. It is better to take one's valuation on a uniform currency basis, and then to issue the frankest warnings against interpreting the difference between two valuations at different levels as indicative of equivalent change of physical assets. It is quite obvious that it would be possible to get an enormous apparent increase of wealth when the actual objects of enjoyment might be identical, by the simple process of multiplying the currency by the printing press.

The False Increase in Capital Values.

Some superficial critics alleged that this was what the Board of Inland Revenue did in their memoranda on the " Increases of War Wealth," whereas it was perfectly clear to anybody studying the matter carefully that they were fully alive to the peculiar character of the increases during the war, for they made repeated reference to increased value *" as expressed in money."* I should like to refer to the evidence that I gave before the Committee myself on this point on the following lines :—

Much criticism centres round the *principle* of the War Wealth Levy. We are told that at first it was " out to get the profiteers," then we found that it was attacking a wider range, namely, the people who were better off than before the war, and then, lastly, that it was still wider, namely, the people who were not *really* better off, but only nominally better off. These are precisely the three stages through which the Excess Profits Duty passed. At first, it was a principle to get hold of the people who made profits *out of the War;* then when this was found impossible, the absolute principle was freely asserted as the basis, viz., " when so many people are worse off during the war it is only right that those who are better off should pay." But it was soon realised that with the depreciation of the currency the retention of the pre-war standard, and a fraction of the excess amounting to fifteen per cent., left a man still worse off in *real* income than he was formerly, and the principle was re-stated, as relative, viz., " We are, of course, all worse off, but some are less so than others, and those must bear the brunt of the burden." In writing of the origin of Excess Profits Taxation in other countries, I have shown that hardly anywhere did the " war profit " idea survive the stage of being a mere impetus to action.

" No one will accuse me, I think, of having written with any prejudice in favour of taxation

by reference to capital. . . . . *If fairly
substantial general allowances are made; we
may be said to be left with a proposal to tax,
in the main, only the third section due to
currency depreciation. This is alleged to be
very reprehensible and indefensible in principle. But is it so clear that it cannot be a
just basis in a special emergency?* It might
conceivably happen that, owing to a sudden
currency expansion, without any trading excess
profits having been made or any other kind of
accretions to capital, the whole nominal value
of existing wealth should be doubled. But it
would only be doubled as a whole—taken on
individual assets it might be very uneven in its
action (for capital values), and, although collectively, people were just as wealthy as
before, taken individually, they would have
changed their relative positions seriously,
and some would be much better off than
others by the change. Is there any serious
objection to such an application of taxation as would pay some regard to this
fortuitous change of relationships, and do
something towards a restoration of the
status quo? This is very much what is
proposed in effect, and the proposal is hardly
so ridiculous or invalid in principle as some
of your witnesses seem to urge. It is dis-
tinctly more equitable than a Capital Levy
in this regard."

The Valuation of Individual Wealth To-day.

Now the method pursued for present purposes of a levy has generally been to get *not* the figure comparable with the national wealth, but the total individual wealth. Still, the lines are approximately the same, leaving out certain categories. The official return estimated for individuals, as at 30th June, 1919, some 4,000 millions increase—this included items which would be similar if included in a full National estimate, *i.e.*, lands and buildings 430 millions, farmers' capital 290, movable property 450 millions, decreases of 1,075 for individual holdings in Railways and foreign securities, etc. There was very little increase except that created through war loans, which, though they may be added to wealth for individual purposes, are taken off for the nation's wealth, as a debt on its property.

But, at the present time, there are at work various economic factors causing great disturbances in capital values ; these disturbances work in different directions in different cases, and they do not necessarily affect income in the same direction or in the same degree. Persons who have in the past invested all their wealth in fixed-interest-bearing securities (such as foreign Government loans or debentures of public companies), find that the capital represented by their securities has greatly decreased

D

in value. The income, however, remains constant and gives no indication of the amount (or even of the existence) of the capital decrease. Again, other persons who have invested their wealth in house property find in many instances a very substantial increase in the value of their capital, but the income derived from it (after making the necessary allowance for the increased cost of repairs) is in many cases smaller than before the war. The decline in the actual income gives no indication of the increase in the capital value ; indeed, it seems to suggest the reverse.

One could fairly assume that left alone, property rents could be double their old level, but this double income would be capitalised on a lower basis owing to the rise in interest and in the net result the capital value is probably not more than 1,200 millions greater.

While I prefer to give no estimate of capital wealth at the present time for the reasons stated, I should like to add that, in my judgment, it cannot *exceed* 19 to 20,000 million £, and is probably much less.

The aggregate of individual wealth has moved from 11,000 millions in 1914 to about 15,000 millions at June 1920. Of course, these are merely expressed in money values—the increase in real or intrinsic values is certainly almost negligible,

CHAPTER II

AT the outset I must remind you of what I have said already upon the main purpose of these lectures, in order that you may not get restless because I stop short of the application of my results to the practical problems of the day. Instead of starting with the data in these controversies as already given, I am considering the data themselves without regard to their subsequent application, to indicate how they are obtained, the extent of their reliability, what they really mean, and the uses to which they can be properly put.

We have already considered the National Wealth under, at any rate, one of its aspects, namely, its aggregate before the war and at the present time, and we have now to consider the National Income. This is a much less difficult and abstract conception in many ways, as it does not depend upon difficult questions of valuation, but can be measured by direct arithmetical methods over a fixed period of time, viz., one year, with which we are all familiar. Nevertheless, it has difficulties of its own in principle, and it has some of the same difficulties in regard to material at the present time as were considered in the last section. Many of the figures upon which we have to rely at present are heavily charged with war conditions, and some of the most important fixed points cannot be, at the moment, clearly discerned owing to the fog of war, and the rapid change in prices and profits.

Ideas of National Income.

We have, first of all, to settle what we really mean by the term " National Income," because different people attach to it different ideas. I define it to be the aggregate money expression of those goods produced, and services performed,* by the inhabitants of the country in a year which are, as a fact, generally exchanged for money. Everything that is produced in the course of the year, every service rendered, every fresh utility brought about, is part of the national income. Thus it includes the benefit derived from the advice of a physician, and the pleasure got from hearing a professional singer. Sir Leo Chiozza Money remarks :—" It is sometimes argued that if the national dividend were better distributed part of it would disappear, since it consists of the valuation of services

---

* Subject to certain reservations—*vide* p. 49 *et seq.*

rendered to the well-to-do."* I have frequently contended that our method tends to exaggerate the value of services amongst the rich :

" It is obvious that if a ring of people like to call their services any given ' value,' there is no real obstacle A., the great surgeon, performs an operation for B., the prima donna ; B. goes to sing at a social function for C., the leading barrister ; C. takes a brief for A. in a lawsuit. Each one is in the habit of selling the particular service to the community at £100, but on this occasion each sends in a bill for £1,000, which is paid, and up goes the national income by £2,700 above its true figure upon any reasonable exchange basis. . . ."

" Exchanges are going on between people upon one plane for services at a valuation belonging to that plane, and never brought into comparison with values on a lower plane. If there were equal redistribution, that plane of values would not exist. . . . If, however, we had a redistribution of existing capital wealth, socialistically, many services would alter in value ; no physician would get differential fees for identical services. But it is a mistake to suppose that the only change would be a reduction of certain values, and, therefore, a reduction in the aggregate. Certain services would rise in value because of the wider

* *The Nation's Wealth* : p. 114 *et seq.*

effective demand. No one can say what the new equilibrium would be—it is an insoluble problem, because only ' broken arcs ' of the demand and supply curves are known to us.

" It is, however, as well to remember that we cannot divide up the aggregate and re-arrange it to the same total, like a box of bricks. It is rather more like the cells of an organism. At the same time it is clearly possible to exaggerate the importance of this point, and the figures we have are sufficiently stable and homogeneous in component exchange values for all ordinary purposes."*

The National " Heap."

I am most anxious that the conception of national income should be a living and real one to you all, and not merely a mass of figures, so, before we leave this, may I put to you a homely and simple and, therefore, perhaps, inexact illustration, which may serve to make the matter more graphic. To many of you the idea will be fairly familiar, to others, perhaps, not so, but if you will really seize it, it will be one key for many other mysteries of production and exchange, and particularly of currency and the payment of war indebtedness. Will you suppose that all the services and goods that are produced by us as a com-

* *British Incomes* : p. 419.

munity in a year are all piled in the centre of this room in a great miscellaneous heap. Every one of you, in the work that you do, is putting that work there. It includes the boots and the clothes that are made, the loaves that are baked, the sheep that are reared, the sermons that are preached, the songs that are sung, the physician's advice, the pilot's skill, the banker's knowledge, the business man's services of organisation, the crossing sweeper's service, indeed, everything that can be given by us whereby we have a claim upon the work of our fellow-men who are contributing to the heap, including the services of those who have helped to make the heap larger than it would or could be if we started afresh without the assistance of piled-up capital goods saved from the heaps of former years. Let it be supposed that we have no such thing as money, but that for each contribution we have made to the heap there is given to us a " labour or services ticket " with a claim to draw something out of the heap in return—if you like, for the moment, equivalent in its labour or equivalent in its skill, or its sacrifice, to what we have put in. The people who have refrained from an earlier consumption on the faith of their title to later consumption somewhat larger in extent, also have their title to the heap. Now the total of tickets giving titles to the heap will exactly equal the mass in the heap, and when we have all drawn out what we want of other people's products and handed in our tickets, the heap will have vanished. It is true that when we present our tickets, we shall, perhaps, in our demands for a particular thing that is in the heap, exceed the actual supply ; in other cases, we may ask less. There may be fewer loaves put upon it than we want, and, perhaps, more servants and third-rate music-hall songs than there is a demand for, but these are questions of bad anticipation of demand, and we must rule them out for the moment. The point is now, that we cannot, as a whole, get more out of the heap than we have put into it. If we each secretly make up our minds one night to put a little less on and say nothing about it to anyone else, we shall all be amazed to see how the heap shrinks in its mass. On the other hand, if all tackle their job in the spirit of Sunny Jim, there will be a magic magnification before us.

A Scotch congregation, anxious to do honour to a beloved parson and show him some mark of their appreciation of his devoted services, sought the most suitable expression for their feelings. After anxious consultations it was decided to present him with a barrel of whisky. As the readiest means of compassing the gift, it was agreed that contributions should be collected in kind, and accordingly an empty barrel was obtained and, at a time and place arranged, the individuals of the flock brought their offerings in vessels of different kinds and duly poured them into the open bunghole, after which the cask was sealed in preparation for the ceremonial of presentation. This great day arrived, with the pomp and panoply of sheriffs, dominies, and officials, and the minister and his family prominent. A most pleasing feature to all was, of course, the necessity for a general sampling of the present, and it was a solemn moment when the senior elder turned the tap. But, lo ! there flowed forth—*pure water* !

When the brilliant idea occurs secretly to each one alike that the niggardly character of his little contribution will be lost in the general fund of honest work, there is likely to be a surprising result !

Now, what happened in the war ? Suddenly, a very large number of contributors to the heap had to leave off putting things upon it, and to go elsewhere to fight. They had still to be fed and clothed, and so the heap had to be kept up in spite of their absence, as they were still drawing subsistence from it. It is a fact that in paying for the war everything had to come out of that heap unless it could be borrowed from other countries. First of all the quantities of life's necessaries in it had to be maintained, and then the character of it had to be vastly altered to include all kinds of armaments and war materials, and the burden of doing this fell upon a comparatively small fraction of the producers. The war could not be paid for and fought out of the heaps of future years, all the talk about making posterity pay for the war, notwithstanding. Everything had to come out of current production. All that was available for war was the difference between what people put on the heap and what they took off it. We had, in consequence, the campaign to take off as little as possible— Economy and Rationing. Then came the campaign to put on as much as possible—overtime, and lady workers emerging from their own homes and leaving little private or domestic heaps—contributions to the public heap by hundreds of wives and young ladies who had never done anything more than make fancy antimacassars. I am afraid that in a few cases some of the latter forgot that the object was to make the heap bigger, and as fast as they put services on it had what they call a " good time," taking from the heap all sorts of things which they had never had before, in the way of furs, restaurant dinners, and expensive amusements. Nevertheless, the principle of addition was clear.

Now the actual work of extracting from the heap the materials for waging the war, had to be done by the State, but, by hypothesis, all the contributors to the heap had tickets for what they had put on, and, therefore, had the right to clear it right out. The State, which was, of course, our " collective will," came along and took from our tickets a certain proportion, according to its own plan, which gave it a title to the heap, and lessened our own title. This was taxation. But the State found that in this way it could not get enough, and so it had a second way and came to us and said, " If you will give up to us voluntarily, some more of your tickets, we promise, when the war is won, to give you a special and exclusive title to an extra bit off future heaps." This, we called Borrowing and War Loans. Still the fund for the State was not enough. What remained to be done ? We can picture now that the State by stealth in the night printed a number of tickets for which no corresponding goods had been put upon the heap—if you like, twice as many tickets—and then when these came into the market with all the others clamouring for their share of the heap, it was very soon clear that there were twice as many tickets as goods, and in the scramble for the diminishing heap, people quite gladly gave two tickets to secure an article where one would have previously sufficed. Then by the time the whole heap was cleared and all the tickets had changed hands, the equivalent of every unit of the heap was practically twice in tickets what it had been before. The goods and the tickets, instead of cancelling out at their unit values cancelled out only if two tickets were offered in place of one. This third method

is what we know as " inflating the currency,"
and I have given you very crudely the quantity
theory of money. Now the State inflates the
currency whenever it uses more purchasing
power than it has withdrawn by taxation, or
borrowing, from the people. It can but deflate
by the opposite method, namely, withdrawing
from the people more purchasing power than it
uses. Thus, with all these tickets in circulation,
the Government might each year, by taxation,
draw a large number from the purchasers, but
when it came to claiming upon the heap for its
own purposes, use only a few of them and
destroy the rest. Then the number of tickets
per unit of goods would become lower than two,
and the process would be continued until the
original number of tickets were available.

Now these tickets are what we refer to as
"money," and in " money " I include not only
currency notes, but also banking forms of credit.
By thinking of all this stream of production
in this way, apart from its value in terms of
money, you will be able to refer most of the
difficult questions relating to national income
to a more sensible test than by dealing with it
in your mind in the abstract. In my third
lecture I shall talk about the distribution of
this heap amongst the different purchasers and
people who give service. I am now only concerned with the measure, in tickets, of its size.
We must have a common denominator ; we

cannot add weights and lengths and sizes. Books may be heavy, but we cannot add them to coal ; sermons and lectures may be long, but we cannot add them to dress lengths ; songs and concerts can be nice, but we cannot add them to vanilla ices ! This common denominator must be our currency, but you will see that the same sized heap can quite easily be expressed by an aggregate of units very widely different from each other according to the number of " tickets " in existence.

There are several matters relating to the computation of national income which are matters of principle, formerly negligible, but now of great importance.

The Household Services of Wives.

First. It has never been the practice to set any value upon the household services rendered by wives to their husbands and homes. If one were evaluating the total worth of all human effort in money—whether such effort were in fact or in custom habitually exchanged for money—no doubt it would be necessary to make an addition under this head. So, equally, would it be necessary to evaluate all the services rendered by individuals in their leisure time to themselves where those services have a commercial value. For example, the task of putting down linoleum and hanging pictures would be an addition to one's income at the rate which that service would cost if paid for in the ordinary way. But, after all, in these matters one must have some sense of teleology. We can allow as a deduction from income expenses incurred in getting that income, but not the various ways of spending the income itself upon the essentials of life. Therefore, we do not allow as a deduction from income the cost of boots, clothing or food. Similarly, we should not allow the cost of keeping a home, because these are not business expenses. Our instinct is sound, therefore, in calculating the net amount of money that passes over the threshold of the home, but ignoring everything that is done within that home itself in the way of services. It is true that the payment to a domestic servant, while it constitutes an addition to the National Income, is no deduction from the income of the employer ; in this sense, therefore, we have only a question of degree, and the point at which we have hitherto stopped may be regarded as illogical. In " British Incomes and Property " I stated :—

" We omit the immense productive services of wives in household duties, of amateur gardeners, of all who spend any effort, outside their main business of money-income or earning, in performing services or making things. If I get the services of a shoeblack, I add two-pence to the national income, but if I black my own shoes and he *gives* me some tangible article or service, the money measure is the same as before, but the national wealth is greater. We are often told we must not reckon things twice, and this warning certainly covers all payments made to earn and to keep income intact. If a man pays a housekeeper £1 a week for her services out of his income of £200 a year, they figure together in the national income at £252, but if he marries her and continues his payment of £1, the national income shrinks by £52. It is imperative that this limitation of the income tax statistics as a representation of the 'national dividend' be borne in mind."

Now, so long as this convention was thoroughly understood, I think it was hitherto a reasonable one, the evaluation of wives' services being so difficult where not actually subject to a monetary test ; but a great strain was thrown upon it during the war. Obviously, if a million women performed services in industry worth £100,000,000 a year, and a million wives stopped at home, we have an addition of £100,000,000 to the national income ; but if these ladies changed places, the million wives going out to work and earning £100,000,000, while the million women became domestic servants and housekeepers in the homes of the wives instead of being out-workers, and are also paid £100,000,000, we get an addition of £200,000,000 to the national income. If there is an important change in social practice over a long period, this principle might be also of importance, but on the whole I think we are reverting gradually to a stable condition of social practice, and that the balance of advantage is to ignore the difficulties raised by this conventional treatment.

Co-operative Incomes.

Second. The extension of co-operative trading tends to diminish the national income as we express it, where the actual services and commodities produced and enjoyed are undiminished. This arises from the fact that in our conception of income at present, we do not include services which have a strong element of "mutuality." Anyone interested in this aspect should read carefully the reports of the Royal Commission on the Income Tax.

Public Services and Taxation.

Third. Any tendency to have services performed by officials paid entirely out of the proceeds of taxation, instead of out of the proceeds of fees and trading charges, tends to swell the amount of the national income. For example, take the services of the telephone for business purposes, ignoring its private use. If this is paid for by fees, they are deducted as a business expense, and do not form a part of profits. But if we were to put the telephone service as a national charge paid for out of the income tax, we should at once transfer it from the class of expense incurred in getting one's income into expenses or ways of spending one's income. Income Tax is not a deduction in computing one's income. The amount of profits assessable and the income received would, *pro tanto*, be increased, and the whole of the telephone service and salaries would form an addition to, or duplication, of national income. The same applies to any municipal services which assist people to get their incomes, and which can be charged as business expenses, but which are transferred to the rates now generally paid by householders. Such rates are not a deduction for assessing income. Therefore, a tramway service, or a telephone service, or an electricity service, or a market service, used for business purposes, and subsidised out of the rates owing to working deficiencies, represents something thrown out of the category of business expenses into the category of personal expenses, and tends to swell the national income wrongly. On balance, no doubt, the profit in relief of rates is greater than the deficiencies.

The Payment of Interest on the National Debt.

Fourth. The foregoing may not seem of much importance, but when we come to consider the present position of taxation in relation to

E

the payment of interest on debt, we shall see that
the same principle is very significant. Everyone who owns less than the average holding of
War Loan is, on balance, paying interest to
his fellows for their net balance of loans to him.
Everyone who on balance holds more War Loan
than the average, is receiving interest on money
he has lent his fellows. Now, in ordinary life,
such transactions would represent an addition
to the incomes of those receiving interest, and a
deduction from the incomes of those paying
interest. If A. lends B. £1,000 at 5 per cent.,
A's income includes £50 of interest, but B.'s
income is diminished by a charge of £50 for
interest. But in the actual way we are now
doing it, the individuals owing the interest do
not pay it *quâ* interest—they pay it *quâ* taxation, into a common pool out of which the
interest is paid. These payments *quâ* taxation
are not allowed as deductions by our conventional method of computing national income.
We take credit for all the pluses, but do not
debit the minuses. The £350,000,000 of
interest paid by one set of inhabitants to the
other, would, if paid as " balance of interest "
transactions, have no effect upon the nominal
national income, but under our method of
paying it out of taxation, we at once increase
the national income, and " the bigger the debt
the bigger the income."

This, therefore, raises the question acutely

whether we have a logical definition of income if we ignore payments for taxes to the extent that we have done in the past. Should we not take out all those payments of taxes which are spent, not upon the objects for which we live, in the normal understanding of " life," but for such an exceptional object as the war, it being found that such payments come in to be counted again as income elsewhere ?   You will remember that in the case of National Capital this is practically what we did. Having counted the debt as income to the holders, we took it from the collective property of the State and individuals remaining. The question now arises whether some such operation should not be performed in computing the national income.

The Difference between Excess Profit Duty and Income Tax.

Fifth. The preceding question is made all the more acute when we consider the difference in treatment between Excess Profits Duty and Income Tax. For the E.P.D. is a business expense and is deducted before the incomes are computed upon which income tax is paid. Unless we can agree that Excess Profits Duty and Income Tax are, so to speak, convertible terms, and should be treated in the same way —which means that we should add the whole of the E.P. Duty to the existing figures of National Income, *or* deduct both E.P. Duty and Income Tax and so alter our practice in regard to the latter—we get a really ridiculous position. Suppose that out of a gross income of £1,000,000,000 the State took £200,000,000 for E.P. Duty and £240,000,000 as Income Tax, the State would take in all £440,000,000 of revenue, leaving individuals with £560,000,000, but the National Income would stand at £800,000,000. Now, let the State say " We still wish to take a revenue of £440,000,000, but we will abolish the E.P. Duty." It then has to raise £440,000,000 upon an assessment of £1,000,000,000, which is a rate of just under 9s. in the £. This leaves the relative positions of the State and individuals as before, but the National Income becomes £1,000,000,000. Any " loading " of the income tax (or rates on households, which are a kind of local income tax) to meet charges hitherto borne out of other kinds of taxes, at once automatically alters the computation of National income.

The Treatment of Pensions.

Does not this again lead to the view that, with the enormous extent of present expenditure, and the present temporary way of meeting it, we must revise our methods and deduct from the gross income, plus Excess Profits Duty, a sum equal to the amount of income paid to individuals as interest which is payable out of taxation.   This amounts to a frank recognition of a distinction between the payment (*via* taxation) by individuals of interest to others, and the payments for taxation, which are spent in the ordinary way upon the consumable " benefits " of life, such as the Navy, the Army, the Police, education, rates, and other current services which we enjoy.   If we decide to do this what ought to be done about pensions ?   I do not mean ordinary Civil Service pensions, because these may be said to be equivalent to salaries, and the pension system is only an alternative to paying a higher salary to those rendering existing services and leaving them subsequently to look after their own superannuation allowance—such pensions must be taken as equivalent (plus the salaries) to the cost of present services.   But pensions for services definitely in the past, having no present counterpart, stand on a different footing.   In this case we have an analogy to the interest which is being paid in respect of entirely past services, and if the pensions are brought into the aggregate of national income, we ought to take the cost of them from the incomes of the income taxpayers.   If this is not done, it will be seen that the more pensioners we have the richer we are, and our figures become meaningless.

How is National Income Estimated in Different Countries ?

There are three main methods :—

(1) *Statistics of Income Taxation.* The value of this method depends on the completeness and efficiency of the tax in question. It is, for example, very different if England is compared with Italy. " Taxation at the Source " obviously gives more complete figures, requiring less supplementing from other sources.

The extent to which this method covers the field depends upon the exemption limit, or the point at which the tax starts. The Prussian limit of £47 per annum enabled the method to be applied to cover the bulk of the population, but the British limit of £160 did not account for as much as one-half of the total income, or more than one-eighth of the people. The American exemption, still higher, left an even greater proportion to be dealt with by other means. But with all its defects, this method is the only really satisfactory one for dealing with the income of the wealthier section of the community.

(2) *The Occupational Census Method.*—This method is used for dealing with the wage-earning classes and smaller incomes where the income tax statistics do not apply. These classes have little income beyond their earnings, and the average earnings of each class are

determined as closely as may be, and applied to the number of earners in each class or occupation as given by the Census. The whole value of this method depends, of course, on the accuracy of the Census, and still more upon the care with which wage statistics are prepared and handled. The lower half of the British estimate is determined in this way with very satisfactory material. The same method is adopted for France, but, by the application of averaged earnings, the result is obtained on rougher lines. In France, moreover, the method was applied to businesses and professions in the absence of income tax statistics.

(3) *"Net Output" or Census of Production Method.*—If the total value of work done or goods produced in a year is determined and the values of the raw materials used are deducted the " added value " may be taken to be the fund which forms the people's income. In the British Census of Production, 1907, the " Net Output " was the gross output (selling value) less the cost of materials used. " It expresses completely and without duplication the total amount by which the value (at works) of the products of the industry taken as a whole, exceeded the cost (at works) of the materials purchased from outside, *i.e.,* it represents the value added to the materials in the course of manufacture." It corresponds, *approximately*, to the balance of a trading account. It

constitutes for any industry the fund from which wages, salaries, rent, royalties and sundry expenses have to be defrayed, the balance being profit (or loss). Mr. Flux showed that the results of the 1907 Census were consistent with the estimates of British National Income obtained in other ways. Giffen in 1903 made an estimate by aggregating the value of goods consumed. This method has hitherto been the chief one for the determination of the incomes of the United States.

In addition we have :—

Interest on Capital.—In a few cases estimates are partly made up, or are checked, by a computation of the average yield upon different classes of capital according to the amount of such capital determined in other ways.

The Income " Census."—This method has been adopted in Australia for 1914-15 at the same time as the Wealth Census for ascertaining National Capital.

The Estimate for the United Kingdom.

Now for the United Kingdom, we have to take the matter in three sections :—

(*a*) The Income brought under review for Income Tax, including that investment income actually reaching exempt people.

(*b*) Wage earners not liable to Income Tax.

(*c*) Non-wage earners not liable to Income Tax (*e.g.*, small shopkeepers).

The Section Liable to Income Tax.

With regard to the first section, taking the year 1914-15, we start with the figure of 985.2 millions, being taxable income with an exemption limit of £160, and after allowing for repairs to property, etc., and depreciation of machinery. This figure will be found in the supplementary tables to " British Incomes and Property."

First as to what it represents. A large part of it relates to the profits of businesses assessed on the average of the three years 1911, 1912 and 1913. These were three of the best years of industry, and were succeeeded, prior to the outbreak of war, by some slight decline, the true extent of which, if the war had not intervened, we do not know, but the actual profits of the year 1914, at the rate for the year before the war, can be said to have approximated closely to this figure. They should not have deviated from it by more than a very small percentage.

My total estimate of the allowance which has to be made in order to reduce legal profits for this purpose to the commercial profits for that year, was £30,000,000. There are a great number of ways in which people imagine that the two things are different, but these, on closer examination, are found not to affect the statistics in the long run. Fourteen of these headings were carefully examined and their true effects shown, and out of them only seven had really any valid effect.   They were

For true losses, to which full effect was not given by the statistics of assessment... ...	£16,000,000
The capital contained in annuities... ...	3,000,000
The expenses of limited companies ...	1,000,000
An annual allowance for costs of pit-sinking in coal mines	2,000,000
The obsolescence of buildings and machinery	5,000,000
The depreciation of fixtures and fittings ...	500,000
Expenses of Brewers' tied houses which (at that time) were not allowed as an expense ...	2,000,000

(Say)   £30,000,000

All the other kinds of alleged differences are ruled out for three classes of reasons :—

(1) Reasons relating to the actual character and method of making allowances, *e.g.*, Bad Debts.

(2) The particularist fallacy ; what may be true of some or all the parts separately, is not necessarily true of the aggregate.

(3) The fact that differences of treatment in point of time are not at the same stage in every case, and that in the aggregate the differences disappear.

The total is reduced by £30,000,000, but we add to it £17,000,000 for evasion and another £20,000,000 for income abroad not remitted home.   This was brought into legal charge in 1914, but it would be unwise to say that the legal change had had its effect upon the assessments at so early a date.   Consequently, I made a complete addition for it, and the total of 985 millions thus becomes 992 millions, to which I should add 30 millions for the under-assessment of farmers in 1914, making £1,022 million in all.

Professor Bowley, in his lecture on " The Changes in the Distribution of the National Income," gets for this section a total of 1,040 millions, but he starts with an estimate of 1,000 million and makes no allowance for some of the special features to which I have referred above.

" Intermediate Incomes."

When we come to the intermediate incomes, the only recent investigation was that by the British Association Committee of 1910, which estimated that there were 4,053 thousand persons in the United Kingdom with incomes not assessed to income tax, who were not generally classed as wage earners, and that their aggregate income was 335 millions with an average of £84. Dr. Bowley, who was very largely responsible for the Committee's work, brought the figure down to the year 1913 as 4,310 thousand persons with an aggregate income of 364 millions, and an average income of £84½.

The British Association estimate proceeded on the lines of taking thirty-one Census occupation groups for which the numbers are known, and assigning to each group an average income with a certain range of possible error. The information as to incomes for the Civil Service, Local Government, the Army and Navy, Clergy, elementary teachers, banks and railway servants, was fairly exact. A good estimate was made by sampling and by questionnaires for clerks and shop assistants. Small farmers were dealt with by way of a reference to the rental values of the farms. For the other classes, careful estimates were made of the probable proportions falling within the income tax sphere, and of the average earnings of the remainder. In the aggregate, the range of possible error, or "modulus," as the Committee called it, was not taken as the sum of the moduli, but by adding squares and taking the square root of the sum. The result was £284,700,000 ± 29,400,000—a range of just over 10 per cent. This sum was supplemented by the income from investments and property belonging to this class.

The Wage Earners.

The national Wages Bill has been estimated from time to time by Professor Bowley in great detail. One of his methods is to take the results of the Board of Trade enquiry (the last volume of which came out in 1912) as a basis. The returns from employers were voluntary, but sufficient information was received from the great majority of trades where the work is done in factories or large workshops, to lead to results accurately representing the average earnings. He says "There is little risk of error in the statement that the average of the week's earnings in ordinary industry in the Autumn of 1911 was £1 9s. for men (over 20), 10s. 6d. for lads and boys, and £1 6s. 3d. for all males. (How archaic all these figures seem already!) In default of other information these averages can be applied, with suitable modifications, to other occupations. By this method a table is obtained with average weekly wages under the broad heads of industry, such as textiles, clothing, etc., for both males and females under 20 years, and over 20 years respectively.

As an independent computation, the *annual* average wages bill of the businesses was divided by the average number employed in a full week. These figures, owing to average illness, and unemployment, are 7 per cent. less than the weekly averages. These figures are then linked up with the occupational census with proper allowances for retired workers and casual workers—data for which are derived from the Labour Department statistics, Friendly Societies, etc. The average annual earnings of males occupied in industries worked out at £57 4s. in 1911, this average being raised by the inclusion of coal mining, and lowered by agriculture. Each industry was obtained separately and the total for 11 million occupied male wage earners brought up to 631 million £, including payments in kind to agricultural workers. Similarly, there was 151 million £ for women, with a margin of error greater than in the case of men, but the total concerned was smaller. The 782 million £ resulting was a trifle below other estimates by Sir Leo Chiozza Money, Sir Thos. Whittaker, and the Fabian Society.

The amount and risk of error in the total is comparatively small by this method, as the items do not all err in excess or defect, but there are some minuses against some pluses. I should like to interject here that the total number of manual wage earners and, secondly, of the intermediate class, including shop assistants and those assessed to income tax, excluding wage earners, were got at piecemeal in other ways and found to square with the total occupied population.

As regards the intermediate section, there are certain auxiliary checks, such as the known values of the shops and business premises occupied by these classes, or the acreage of small farms, which considerably assist in determining the accuracy.

The third section overlapped slightly with the income tax assessments, but in 1913 only to a limited extent, viz., about 50,000 persons,

Excluding shop assistants, and allowing for an increase in numbers and rates of wages, Dr. Bowley estimated 770 millions in 1913 as the earnings of 15,200,000 wage earners. This duly allows for unemployment, sickness, holidays and irregular work. Dr. Bowley, when estimating the changes in the National Wage Bill from time to time, has found it more accurate to work from a particular year by the application of factors for changes in rates and numbers to get the figures for other years, than to make direct estimates for such years. He takes the year 1906 as the basis of the measurement of change, because in that year special information was collected by the Board of Trade, which they studied together with the Census of Production in the following year.

The Aggregate Pre-War Estimate.

In aggregating these three sections the first one is the figure of 1,022 million £ for the income tax section, 365 million £ for the intermediate section, and 762 million £ for the wages section (excluding those charged to income tax) or a total of 2,149 million £. We have to add the " unearned " income of those with incomes under £160, old age pensions, and certain other small items, amounting altogether to a little over 100 million £. It should be remembered that this figure includes a certain amount of income or yield which does not go to individuals, but to collective bodies such as charities, to the reserves of public companies, and so on. Very careful and detailed consideration has to be given to the question of how much should be deducted if we are to get the individual figures, for where we desire to have an aggregate of individual tax-paying capacity, the difference is important. (This matter will be dealt with in discussing the distribution of income, but the warning is given here, as it is so frequently overlooked.) It will be seen that this estimate of the national income before the war of, say, 2,250 millions, is considerably less than the 2,400 millions given by some writers, who, possibly, however, intend to allow for renewals and depreciations, out of this higher total. As long ago as fifty years there was a " rule of thumb " method of getting at the national income by doubling the amount assessed for income tax. This was rough and ready, but it is remarkable how near the truth it has remained. You will see that in our calculation it is a trifle less than one-half. The rule has been applied somewhat regardless of adjustments such as I have made to get " pure income," and also of changes in the level of exemption from £150 to £160, but this latter change has served to keep the rule somewhere near the truth, for if the exemption limit had remained at £150, a larger number of wage earners would have been included in the tax returns, and the national income would not have been *quite* equal to twice the income tax figure, before the deductions for repairs, etc.

You will agree that if the national income is the money expression of the value of national produce after allowing for that part of the produce applied to repairs and renewals, there would be an alternative way of discovering the total value of produce for exchange and consumption. This would consist of valuing the total production and deducting therefrom the value of raw materials purchased from abroad, etc., with our existing working capital. The difference would represent the net additional value created and available to be used as income. This very method has been used in the report on the Census of Production in 1907, where the national income is estimated by the addition to the values of goods produced of services and net imports, to give an approximate net profit. The computation was as follows :—

INCOME, 1907.   £ millions.

Gross output of industry, mining and agriculture excluding duplication, but including imported materials to value of £380 millions	1370
Carriage, merchanting and retailing of home-goods	430
Duties on home-goods	50
Imports ready for consumption, valued at ports ..	220
Duties on carriage, merchanting and retailing of imports	140
	2210

F

		Brought forward				2210
Subtract exports	..	..	..	..	..	465

Total value to purchasers of material goods available for consumption, maintenance of capital or saving 1745

Subtract maintenance of plant, etc. (£175 millions) and of consumers' stock (£15 millions) .. 190

Remainder, available for consumption or saving .. 1555

Add value of personal services and occupation of houses 375

Add new investments abroad 100

Total Income £2030

While this is admittedly rough, it indicates that the other method cannot be very wide of the truth, and I should think we are perfectly safe in saying that it cannot be wrong by as much as 10 per cent., *i.e.*, the national income before the war *could* not have been more than £2,450,000,000, nor less than £2,050,000,000, and almost certainly lay between 2,200 and 2,300 million £.

THE NATIONAL INCOME TO-DAY.

At this date (February, 1921) we have no very clear idea as to the actual number of people engaged in industry, though, of course, we know how many come within insured classes under the extended schemes. Still less do we know the

numbers in the separate industries, and any
information we have as to the increase in piece-
work rates or time rates is difficult to apply,
because these fundamental facts are missing at
present. The Census result will help to re-
solve many doubts, as it will give us a new
and more secure basis on which to work. The
lowering of the exemption limit to £130 at a
time when there has been a general increase
of wages has brought a very large number into
this class of official statistics. Formerly, the
Income Tax statistics were almost clear of
weekly wage-earners, but now some four million
at least come within the figures. Let us look
at the matter very broadly, assuming, what is
very nearly true, that there is no information
about total wages. Even if we had the task
of disentangling the Income Tax figures, it is
not easy to determine the overlapping. The
most important statistical return yet given—
to which reference will be made again—is that
rendered to the Royal Commission on Income
Tax and included in the Appendix, p. 90, where
the total taxable income of the Income Taxpayers for year to March, 1919, is given as 2,072
million £.* To a considerable extent the figure
is conditioned by the profits of the years 1915,
1916 and 1917, which were the average for the

* The later figures published in the Report of the Commissioners
of Inland Revenue have been substituted for those given to the
Royal Commission.

assessment—the first two were taxable partly at 50 per cent., but for the most part at 60 per cent., and the last at 80 per cent. on the excess for Excess Profits Duty.

Now, if the revenue had been obtained by Income Tax instead of Excess Profits Duty, the assessed profits would have been higher by the amount of the Excess Profits Duty, assessed on the average of these three years, unless, indeed, we assume that it was merely added to profits, and not a tax on profits at all. Then the amount of Income Tax evasion was becoming very considerable indeed, far greater than before the war, and between the two, I think the total profits assessable to Income Tax, excluding Excess Profits Duty, could not have been far short of 2,400 million £. Now the Income Tax was supposed at one time to "divide" the national income into approximately two halves, but that was with exemption at £160. From the return 373 million £ belonged to the class between £130 and £160, and so the amount belonging to the classes over £160 would be 2,030 million £, and if the pre-war ratio between taxable income and total income still held good, the total, after taking away the Excess Profits Duty payments as not actual income, would be some 3,950 to 4,050 million £. But, of course, when quite a large part of the population has, so to speak, marched past the fixed £160 mark, this cannot be a good test, otherwise when decreases in money values had pushed all but one man beyond the £160 mark, we should be assuming that that one man had an income equal to all the tax payers. So a little closer approach is suggested.

We know that before the war the " top " 1,2 0,000 of the population between them had 1,022 million £ assessed. What do the top 1,240,000 receive in 1918 according to this new table ?

From a total of	5,747,000 we may
take the three classes up to £250 ..	4,490,000
leaving	1,257,000
and deduct as standing at £250 another	13,000
We have left	1,244,000
people whose total income is	£2,400 million.
less the amount appropriate to the classes deducted above	724
or,	1,676 million £.

Now assuming the *distribution* of income has remained fairly steady—an assumption to be examined presently—it can be said that the national income has increased in the same proportion as this top section. In this case the total, after deduction of Excess Profits Duty paid, would be in the neighbourhood of 3,650 million £, which was probably much nearer the truth.

After these rough approaches, let us try a still closer method, and rely on the official statistics we have as far as they take us, that is for 5,747,000 taxpayers, carrying us deep down into the weekly-wage earning class to include those who are best off amongst them. We have to estimate for the *remainder* of the inhabitants only. How many workers were there in 1920 to correspond with the 20,700,000 before the war ? We remember that we had enormous war losses, and a considerable section of the population has been withdrawn from industry by death and disablement. We also know that the volume of production in 1920 was still far below the good trade years 1912 and 1913, but, of course, we can put this down to a lower average output per person. Against these evidences of reduced numbers we can urge the natural increase of the population, the cessation of emigration, the fact that the tide of new female labour set up during the war, has by no means fully receded, and the still more obvious evidence of the intense pressure upon our existing housing accommodation. Some may fairly conclude that the number of incomes is not *less* than the old fig u of 20,700,000, and may well be greater. Let us assume for the moment it is the same—what is the average income of the 14,903,000 ?

If we plot out the facts on a Pareto line—and there is no good reason for distrusting its indications altogether—the 20,700,000th wage would fall at £83—and the average income of the class " £83 to £130 " would be almost £93, giving an aggregate for this whole class of £1,430,000,000, and a National Income of about 3,500 to 3,600 million £. Now I am disposed to think the Pareto index would be rather higher, except for a very poor section not receiving wages, and that the average wage will be nearly £100, making the total 3,600 to 3,700 million £ for 1918-19.

As regards the movement of profits since 1918-19, the total Income Tax assessment for 1919-20 was in the neighbourhood of 2,200 millions and probably some 100 millions of the difference applied to weekly wages, so that I feel that we may put the National Income conjecturally (computed on the old principles) at 3,900 million £. Now this may easily be 200 or 300 millions out, but my feeling is that it is certainly not less than 3,700 millions and may *possibly*, though it is not likely, be over 4,100 million £, although estimates made by way of guesses at the present compared with pre-war production raised by the index number of prices lead to higher results.

Sir Leo Chiozza Money gave an estimate of 3,610 million £ to the Royal Commission on Income Tax for 1920, arrived at by a direct estimate of wage earners' incomes, and in which he included 350 million £ for Excess Profits Duty, so that he was somewhat lower than my figures. I criticised some of the items and the principles adopted, but did not dissent materially from the final result. Allowing the Excess Profits Duty as a deduction at the end is roughly equivalent to the principle for which I have contended, viz., to reckon the full income as assessable, but to allow a deduction for so much of the taxes paid as would be utilised for war loan interest, and brought again into the incomes assessed.

CHAPTER III

WE have now to consider how wealth is held by different proportions of the population, and how this holding is changing.

It is only of recent years that we have been able to form reasonably accurate ideas upon the subject, but now, thanks to the super-tax and the system of abatements that have obtained in the last few years, we can divide the total assessed income into groups which fit all the data so exactly that one can, for ordinary purposes, quite afford to ignore any possible margin of error.

Scientific Spirit Essential.

My usual preface is, I am afraid, particularly necessary on this occasion. You will realise that, in asking what we know statistically on this subject, we are getting much nearer than we have so far ventured to the real problems and polemics of the day. Some will be eager to draw what, according to their political and social leaning, they consider to be inevitable conclusions, and to use them in support of their ideas for improving the world, or preventing it being destroyed. I have no concern here with that part of the matter, as the task of examining the facts in as colourless and as dispassionate a way as possible and without the inevitable leanings that come from pre-conceived though honest policies, is a task quite enough to fill the place and time of a Newmarch Lecturer, and better in keeping with his academic surroundings.

Tests of Distribution.

Time need not be greatly taken up with the question of methods of testing or expressing changes in distribution. All the simpler statistical terms have their drawbacks. The handy " average " is not much to lean upon—the average rises when the whole mass of money income rises, without any relative changes in the parts or proportions. The average may remain the same even though there are important changes in distribution over a period. For example, there may be an extra income of £100,000 balanced by 1,000 incomes which have been reduced by £100 each—and this would give no change in the average. Again the mode is useless, and the distribution does not follow the " normal law of error," like a natural or biological series—that is with a curve like a cocked hat or sugar loaf— but is asymmetrical to a degree. The median or middle person of the series tells us little, though if we combine it with the upper and lower quartiles we get a much better notion of the facts. Thus, if we say roughly that the person occupying a place along the scale one quarter up the series has an income such and such a fraction of the income of the middle person of the series, and that the person three-fourths of the way up has an income so many times the middle one, we can get a fair test of the distribution at one time compared with another, because it is a good measure of the *slope*, like Pareto's line. A view that, I believe, is shared by Dr. Bowley, is that a good way to measure social changes over a period of time is to fix on the upper decile (*i.e.*, the man who stands one-tenth of the way down the series) and examine the conditions always at that point. Before the war the upper decile was just on the border line of being liable to income tax. I think to-day too, with the revised limits of exemption for "man and wife," he is in about the same position. But for present purposes we shall keep mainly to percentages, *i.e.*, that such a percentage of the total number receives such a percentage of the total income, and this method, I hope, will satisfy you all.

Pareto's Line

I should explain that in the Pareto test we take statistics of the number of incomes above certain amounts something in this way. On a squared sheet we plot the high incomes up at the top left hand, showing on a level with the vertical scale at £100,000 the number of incomes above that figure ; then on a level with £10,000 the total number above that, and so to the smaller incomes and much larger number of persons. When these points are joined they will be found in a Pareto distribution to lie practically on a straight line. The details plotted are not the actual numbers, but the logarithms of the numbers. If we plot the actual numbers we get a curve, but taking the logarithms of the numbers gives virtually a straight line, which enables us to fill up any particular gap or ascertain intermediate points. If you look at this Pareto line, the dotted line illustrates the straight line and the black line the actual statistics of incomes as given in the returns to the Royal Commission on Income Tax, and you will see it exhibits a tendency to fall off when it gets towards impossible or " inhumanly " high incomes. The little differences between the actual and the straight lines may be either technical or genuine deviations from the true Pareto line ; we do not know. It is introduced here to show you one of the simpler ways of

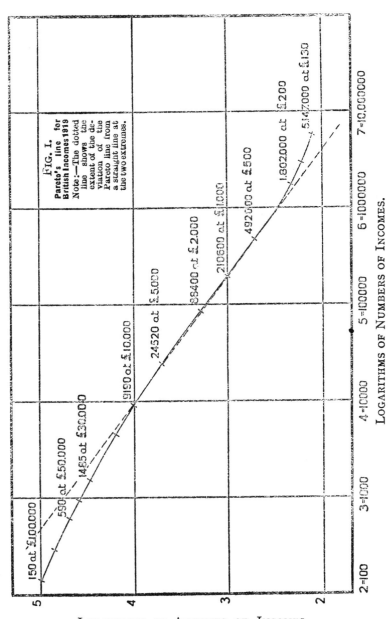

FIG. I.
Pareto's line for British Incomes 1919
Note:—The dotted line shows the extent of the deviation of the Pareto line from a straight line at the two extremes.

150 at £100,000
590 at £50,000
1485 at £30,000
9190 at £10,000
24520 at £5,000
88400 at £2,000
210600 at £1,000
492000 at £500
1,802,000 at £200
5,147,000 at £130

LOGARITHMS OF NUMBERS OF INCOMES.

LOGARITHMS OF AMOUNTS OF INCOMES.

2=100 3=1000 4=10000 5=100000 6=1000000 7=10,000,000

testing distribution. The direction of the line is expressed by a certain figure called " alpha," which is, so to speak, an index. A common figure for " alpha " is 1.6 or 1.7. One can test the slope of the whole distribution at different periods of time for different countries in this way.

Pareto as a Practical Guide.

I may interject, as an interesting reminiscence, that in 1913, when the super-tax statistics were first published, following upon the introduction of that tax, they gave us for the first time an official statement about total incomes over a certain range. I was eager to apply the Pareto rule or formula that I had seen used for other countries to know how it compared with other figures. I annoyed my colleagues at the Revenue in charge of this administration very much by telling them that they had " missed " over a 1,000 payers in the lowest class, £5,000 to £10,000, and they thought I should be much more usefully employed in telling them *who* they were ! However, they promptly went and found them, and now you will find that the £5,000 fraternity " toe " the Pareto line quite nicely. As a matter of fact, you frequently find that the Pareto test with any such set of income statistics drops off a little at the bottom. When I got to the £5,000 point I thought it ought to have been on the line, but it was not. So on the theory that in fact it really *was* there, I gave the number of missing incomes. You will find this failure to come up to the correct or logical number at the lowest scale is quite a common feature of tax systems with an exemption limit, for reasons which will be clear to anyone with administrative experience.

The distribution between income classes has always been a most difficult computation, only to be made with great study and care. When the abatements ran up to incomes of £700 per annum and the super-tax was imposed, we were put in possession of details covering a large part of the field of distribution, but leaving the incomes between £700 and £5,000 as unknown factors. However, by such mathematical devices for interpolation as Pareto's formula, it was quite possible to fill up the gap, although certain difficulties arose which were finally found to be due to the fact that the aggregation of individual returns will never equal the whole income arrived at by direct assessment at the source. There was always too much assessed income to be distributed over the scale, so that if there were allotted to the super tax area merely what was assessed to super tax, and to the incomes up to £700, what appeared on the individual returns for those cases, the result was to get so much for the intervening section that the distribution bulged badly, and in a way that mathematical instinct told one must be wrong. It was necessary, in any case, to make a substantial deduction for income that could not go to individuals, such as that flowing to clubs, charitable institutions, municipalities, co-operative societies, etc. This " non-personal " income was the subject of much discussion, and for some time recently 50 or 60 millions was allowed. But of late years, it has been recognised that even this deduction did not get over the difficulty. The total yielded by taxation at the source must always be in sharp contrast to the total of individuals' returns. Thus if a company makes £100,000 and puts £20,000 to reserve permanently, and pays £80,000 in dividends, the £100,000 appears in the Income Tax total, but individual returns will never show the sums put to reserve at all (except so far as they may some day come out in equalising dividends) and some considerable fraction of the dividends will be omitted by individuals in their statements of total income, for which there is relatively much greater opportunity for evasion. Such evasion does not avail for Income Tax, but it might, perhaps, under the old regime, in some cases, have secured larger abatements. It does affect super tax in the large cases, and this is where most of the missing income might be. But it always makes bad statistics.

I remember Dr. Bowley made an ingenious attempt to get over the difficulty. He took the super tax statistics as determining the Pareto line and then continued the line downwards, where it ought to be met by a similar line coming from the abatements. But, instead of that, the lines come parallel. Then follows a kind of " Hunt the Slipper." If you went to the Income Tax statistics and enquired " Where are these people who seem to be mlssing ?" the people at the top said, " You will find the income at the lower end," and when you went down to the people at the bottom they alleged that it was up at the top. Writers using these statistics generally conveniently push this part of the missing assessed income to the end where they would like it to be for the purpose of their argument. We can now get over the difficulty by deducting from the total assessed income a proper sum for income that for one reason or another does not get stated on individual income returns.

When all is said, however, the distribution secured by these devices is tolerably near the truth. It is checked in turn by taking the House Duty statistics, and fitting taxpayers into houses, on the assumption that certain rentals are usually associated with incomes of a certain size, according to common knowledge. This method was adopted by Sir Leo Chiozza Money originally in " Riches and poverty " very successfully for his main lines of argument.

Putting the taxpayers into their houses is a fascinating statistical game reminiscent of " pigs-in-clover," or the *Daily Mail* puzzle, and many perils await the unwary investigator.

The Official Table of Distribution.

When the Royal Commission on the Income Tax met, the Board of Inland Revenue were induced to put forward a complete distribution for the first time, of the whole assessed income for 1919, amounting to 2,073 millions. Here they deduct 230 million £ as other income, viz., non-personal income and incomes accruing to non-residents, *i.e.*, increasing company reserves accounting for the bulk, interest on invested funds of insurance companies, profits and dividends going to residents out of the United Kingdom, with other items for clubs, etc. They stated that this whole sum was subject to a considerable margin of error. The whole estimate is the most reliable possible index to distribution of annual income that we can expect, as it had to be reconciled with the numbers of abatements, the numbers of super tax payers in each class, the yield of super tax, and the total yield of income tax, together with the income charged at different rates below the full 6s. in the £. Any estimate that can satisfy all these demands cannot be far from the truth.

Constancy of Distribution.

In 1914 some 8 per cent. of the total income of the country belonged to a very small fraction, less than one-tenth of one per cent. of the receivers of incomes. The next 22 per cent. in amount went to 1 per cent. of the number of incomes, and the next 15 per cent. of amount of incomes to $4\frac{1}{2}$ per cent. of the people receiving incomes. This amounts to 45 per cent. of the incomes going to about $5\frac{1}{2}$ per cent. of the people with separate incomes. Now the money levels of the incomes may alter, but these proportions have remained approximately constant. What I may call the " slope " of distribution has not materially altered, and, although all classes may have become better off, they have kept their relative positions and proportions with remarkable stability so far as we can test. I have explained the significance of the Pareto index—it is not a perfect measure of distribution, but it is simple, and serves for this purpose. We have had from 1842 till recent years, a classified tabulation of assessments on profits and salaries to which I have applied this test, and found no evidence of any permanent material shifting in the proportions. We have also had at various intervals, classifications of house values—for example, the houses of £50 in rental value increased in thirty years in about the same proportion as the population, and those of £80 rather less. Although the rich have become richer in one sense, I have not been able to find clear signs of increasing concentration of the total wealth in their hands.

It is clear that there is great inequality of distribution, but I agree with Dr. Bowley when he stated " The constancy of so many of the proportions and rates of movement found in the investigation seems to point to a fixed system of causation, and has an appearance of inevitableness."

When we look at the distribution in all the civilised countries that we know, and we find this peculiar characteristic distribution exhibited by the graph with slight differences, one wonders whether it is in the nature of the universe that it should be so, and our minds go back to the middle ages when the community seemed to consist of very rich barons and a lot of wealthless serfs, and we wonder whether the present kind of distribution could have obtained in that age.

In Dr. Bowley's study, which was based upon the data I have already referred to, he concluded " the broad results of this investigation are to show that the national dividend increased more rapidly than the population in the generation before the war, so that average incomes were quite one-third greater in 1913 than in 1880 ; the increase was gained principally before 1900, since when it barely kept pace with the diminishing value of money. The increase was shared with remarkable equality among the various economic classes. Property obtained a diminishing share of the home product, but an unchanged share of the whole income when income from abroad is included.

"The only marked alteration that has been found is the increase of the intermediate class that contains persons with small salaries, profits, or earnings in other forms than wages. These include clerks and others in retail and wholesale distributive trade, and the younger or less successful persons in teaching and other professions.

"Manual labourers have been a diminishing proportion of the population. More of the whole effort of the population has turned to direction, distribution and exchange, and relatively less to production. This has been rendered possible, it may reasonably be presumed, by the increasing services of capital to production, and probably also by the increased intelligence of labour."

A Comparison over an Interval of 120 *Years.*

I should like to refer now to a comparison over a much longer period of time.

It is a remarkable fact that we have no such official return for 120 years, *i.e.*, since the time when the first Income Tax was introduced. For 1801 a classification was given showing all the incomes assessed, from £60 a year to £5,000 a year, and the amount over £5,000 ; or 75 millions in all.* There is no doubt that this total assessment was far below the true mark, because as soon as the " income-tax-at-the-source " system was introduced, the yield of the tax showed an immense leap. It is, therefore, not much of a guide to aggregate income— probably in the lower levels of income many thousands did not come within the assessment at all. But for those who were too conspicuous to be missed, even on a brand new system in its first year of operation, there is nothing to indicate that evasion or under-statement was relatively greater at one stage of income than at another, and if there was x per cent. of evasion all the way down, the *relative* sizes of the classes would not be very different from what they would have shown if the full incomes had been assessed.

Although one may be able to allege, as I did, on my first inspection of the super tax statistics, that a certain class was deficient, it only means that that particular class is deficient in relation to the rest. The whole line may be deficient throughout. If evasion is anything like constant throughout the whole line—and

* Vide *British Incomes* : p. 514.

there is no reason in the ordinary way to suppose it is not—then you do not really substantially alter the slope by getting the true aggregate
figures.

We shall at once ask the question : How has
distribution changed for the people with incomes above the taxable limit ? It is an
interesting question and the answer is very
interesting too. For special technical reasons
I do not go below £200 a year, and I can put
the two distributions side by side in large
classes, 1801 against 1920, and express the
parallel in percentages of the total income over
£200 and £500 respectively. Of the total
number of people with incomes over £200 per
annum in 1801, the £200 to £500 class were
61.5 per cent., now 71.3 per cent. ; the £500 to
£1,000 class were 21.3 per cent., now 15.8 per
cent. ; the £1,000 to £2,000 class 10.3 per cent.,
now 7.8 per cent. ; the 2,000 to 5,000 class
were 5.3 per cent., now 3.7 per cent. ; the
over £5,000 class were then 1.4 per cent., now
1.3 per cent. ; in this sense there are now
relatively fewer rich people, for each class, save the
lowest, is now a smaller percentage than before.
But this result is entirely due to the present
preponderance of the £200 to £500 class.
Perhaps it is to-day easier to bring in these
people to assessment than it used to be in 1801,
and the numbers then may have been exception-
ally defective. Let us assume that condition, and

deal only with the total number having incomes of over £500 per annum. Then we get a remarkably close parallel.

The £500 to £1,000 class were .. 56% now 55.2%
The £1,000 to £2,000 ,, ,, .. 26.3% ,, 27.3%
The £2,000 to £5,000 ,, ,, .. 13.9% ,, 13.0%
The over £5,000 ,, ,, .. 3.8% ,, 4.5%

This indicates that the people with over £500 a year are distributed in income classes practically the same now as they were then. But if we look at the *amounts* of income in the classes, the results are rather different, for there is *relatively* a larger sum in the hands of the " over £5,000 " class, than there was then. Taking, first, the total incomes of all with over £200 a year. The £200—£500 class had 24 per cent. then, 29 per cent. now ; the £500—£1,000 class had 18.6 per cent. then, now 15.8 per cent. ; the £1,000 to £2,000 class had 17.7 per cent, then, and 15.4 per cent. now ; the £2,000—£5,000 had 20.3 per cent. then, and 15.4 per cent now ; the " over £5,000 " class had 19·5 per cent. then, and 24.2 per cent. now. You get the curious result that the three intermediate classes held a far greater proportion then than now, but the "under £500 " and the " over £5,000 " classes held much less. So far as the " under £500 " class is concerned, this may again have been a peculiarity of assessment, that is, relatively greater evasion in that class. So I will again analyse only the total

income in the classes £500 and upwards. The
£500 to £1,000 class had 24.4 per cent. and
now 22.3 per cent. ; the £1,000—£2,000 class
was 23.2 per cent., now 21.8 per cent. ; the
£2,000—£5,000 was 26.7 per cent. now 21.8
per cent. ; the " over £5,000 class " was 25.7
per cent., now 34.1 per cent. This result is
consistent with the following theoretical solu-
tion : The total nominal income has increased
much more than the total population—the
increase has surged upwards through all the
fixed classes, so that there is a smaller population in the ranks of the poorest, with a
nominal income of say under £80 a year, and many
more in the over £5,000 class, but the *slope* of
distribution, *i.e.*, the *relation* between one section
or class and another, has hardly altered. Let us
examine this in the light of the total numbers
and sums assessed. The population subjected
to the tax law has increased not quite five
times, but the people with incomes over £200
have increased on these tables 25 times, and
their income 24 times ; even if we suppose the
old tables were only half the truth, there is an
increase in numbers and income of 12½ times,
or 2½ times the rate of the increase in population.
If we take those over £500, the numbers are
19 times, and the income 22 times as great,
and halving these again, for precaution, we
have, roughly, an increase at twice the rate of
increase of the population.

The General Improvement in Wealth.

Mulhall's old estimate of the national income for 1800 was 230 millions, which, in my judgment, is on the high side. Let us compare that with an estimate, similarly on the high side, of 2,300 millions before the war. Again you get a tenfold increase, compared with fivefold in population, or twice as great. I think this result is as nearly true as one can gather, But the point I now want to make is that the evidence goes to show this increase has been evenly shared by *all* classes of the population.

Now, let us look at the level of prices in 1801. The index number of prices for 1801, compared with 1913 was, roughly, as 235 to 115, or, say, twice as great. That is the order of magnitude of the change. These old index numbers are only comparable by such large multipliers as two or three times ; one cannot go into decimals upon them. There you have clear evidence from the line of statistics and research that the proportion of 235 to 115, or, say, two to one, is the relation of the prices in 1801 to those of 1913. When we combine these two factors, we reach as a broad result a statement that I have often made, but that has frequently caused surprise, viz., " that the ordinary person of to-day is four times as well off in real commodities as the person in the corresponding stage in the scale in the beginning of the

19th century. The bulk of this advance was secured in the first part of the century.

This has a somewhat important bearing, which I will not go into now, on the relativity of the whole idea of the standard of life ; the " living wage " is relative to the age in which one lives, and the general distribution of wealth, and it is obviously relative also country by country.

I may say that I have tested the slope of income distribution by reference to the magnitude of Income Tax assessments in classes,* and of house rentals in classes at various points during the century, and have found no material difference, though there have been little shifts each way from time to time.

Post-War Distribution.

For 1919 I compute that about one twelfth of the gross total income was received by about one 480th of the people, and one-half by approximately one-ninth to one-tenth of the people. But taxation greatly alters these proportions.

Pooling the Surplus Income.

It is important to consider what the division of the income would mean if a levelling down took place, if, for example, all the incomes in

---

* For the difference between this test and the classification of incomes, vide *British Incomes*, pp. 238–256.

excess of £250 per annum were pooled over the whole population. The immediate division is capable of some rough statistical determination, but the division in following years is much more difficult. The difficulties are quite apart from the incomes that would " dry up "—larger earned incomes which the earner would not continue to strive for if he had to take a less reward. There are a good many sources of income or profit which only yield their present income, because of the existence of the " better off " classes, *e.g.*, large houses would fall seriously in value because of less effective demand, and taxi-cabs would be less abundant. Taking, first, the equal division at present, after allowing for the taxation borne by this section, and assuming the public services to be maintained and also that the same relative proportion of national income is set aside for capital extensions, increased production, etc., as before the war, the 1919 income divisible would not exceed 150 millions, which would not give each family more than £14 a year rise, or, say, 5s. a week. I do not think the figure can be more than this, but it may quite possibly be less. Immediately following the division for the following year, I will assume that the people rendering personal services to the rich find employment in meeting the demands set up by the increased purchasing power of those who have received these additional sums. But we have to estimate for the shrinkage in the large earned incomes, in large residential property values, and for the demands on the general public set up by the shrinkage in the local rates reckoned thereon, and the actual reduced money expressions of services rendered to the well-to-do (assumed to be still rendered to them in their reduced circumstances). This task is getting away from statistics to guesswork, but I think we cannot be exaggerating if 100 millions is deducted in respect of these shrinkages for the first year or two. In these circumstances, the increment to the ordinary family might be £5 a year or a little less.

A rough approach to the subject as for 1919-20 would be :—

	Millions £
Taxable income for Income Tax, plus an amount for evasion, assumed to be 1919–20	2,300
Deduct —	
Included for corporations, charities, etc., say ..	150
	2,150
Deduct—	
For the classes up to £250 per annum	740
	1,410
Deduct—	
Taxes now to be paid out of this income ; Income Tax, Super Tax, etc. (but **not** E.P.D.) ..	500
	910

Brought forward		910
Leave thus 1,240,000 people with £250 level out of this		=310
		600
Less Savings required on a pre-war proportion and hitherto made by these classes as a minimum*		
From 350 to		450
From 250 to		150

For 10½ million families this would give an amount from (under) £24 to £14 a year as a *maximum* and possibly much less.

*[The Savings in the pre-war period were £350 to 400 millions.   On the present scale of money this would equal at least .. 750

But some may prefer to write it down to.. 600

It can be urther reduced by repayment of debt made out of E.P.D. or taxes reserved above, and savings by classes other than Income Tax payers .. .. .. 300 to 250

450   350]

We, therefore, get something of the order of 5s. a week to be added to each family, or, perhaps, a little more. Personally, I do not think there would be any more. Probably a little less would be divisible even in the first approach to the subject, and subsequently it would probably diminish.

Some of you may have read that the effect of spreading the Alps with all their majestic mass and volume over the whole of Europe would be to affect the level of Europe by a few inches only. Similarly the effect of spreading such a mass as the Himalayas over Asia, would be to raise the plains very slightly.

Mr. W. H. Mallock, dealing with the question of the effect of a distribution of capital recently, has contended that after the recipients have assumed their new duties as savers, the worker would have only an addition of £4 to his spending resources per annum. But, as Mr. Mallock is generally regarded as a strong partisan, I would prefer to quote in support of my own conclusions, the results of Professor Bowley's recent analysis from a different angle—that of average income : " Only £200 to £250 millions remain, which, on the extremest reckoning, can have been spent out of home-produced income by the rich or moderately well-off on anything of the nature of luxury. This sum would have little more than sufficed to bring the wages of adult men and women up to the minimum of 35s. 3d. weekly for a man and 20s. for a woman, which Mr. Rowntree in ' The Human Needs of Labour ' estimates as reasonable.

" In fact, the spendable wealth of the nation derived from home industry has been grossly exaggerated by loose reasoning. Before the war the home income would not have yielded more than £230 gross annually per family of five, or £170 net after all rates and taxes were paid and an adequate sum invested in home industries. The average family is not, however, five, as is frequently assumed, but about $4\frac{1}{2}$ persons, the number of households is not 9,000,000, as just taken, but about 10,000,000, and the average net income of a family would have been £153 from home-product, or £162, if income from abroad is included. If this sum is compared with pre-war wages, it must be remembered that there are, on an average, nearly two earners to a family.

"An equal distribution of pooled income would make enormous differences to prices, but it does not seem necessary to attempt any estimate here.

"When it is realised that the whole income of the nation was only sufficient for reasonable needs if equally divided, luxurious expenditure is seen to be more unjustifiable even than has commonly been supposed, and the problems of obtaining a distribution that is more reasonable and of reducing poverty appear more difficult, though none the less urgent."

How is our Capital Wealth Held?

Information upon this subject is mainly derived from the Estate Duty Statistics, with the mysterious statistical puzzle known as the "multiplier," which has been the subject of much useful study of late years. The latest information on this was given by the Board of Inland Revenue in their memoranda on the Taxation of War Wealth. The wealth in the hands of individuals that would " come out " on individual returns, was accepted at my figure of £11,000 millions, as in 1914. The Board estimated a net increase in this class of 4,000 million £, which was 5,525 million £ for items of increase, less 1,525 million £ the aggregate of individual items of decrease.* But the increases were not all in the hands of one group, and decreases in the hands of another—there were many people who had enjoyed an increase in one part of their capital, and had a decrease in another (such as their preference holdings). Out of the aggregate decreases of 1,525 million £ they estimated 500 million £ belonged to persons who had decreases as a whole, the remainder belonging to people who had a net increase in their total estates. So they had to classify an increase for the latter class of 4,500 million £, or 4,180 million £ after deducting the value of furniture and residences. They gave a table, based on Estate Duty Statistics and Super Tax samples, which accounted for this

* This referred to the state of affairs as at June, 1919, and was materially less than the estimate I made, during the war, of the probable increase after the end of the war at a date unknown. But at this date (December, 1921) a large part of the increase has disappeared through altered values.

H

4,180 million £ increase, and for a total post-war amount of 13,046 million £. If the remaining 2,000 million £ (approximate) belonging to the "new poor" were spread on the same line of distribution we should have :—

Million £.				Fortune in £.
4555				under 5000
1217	held by	169040	..	to 10,000
2202	,,	138460	..	,, 25,000
1731	,,	48810	..	,, 50,000
1432	,,	20570	..	,, 100,000
1615	,,	11200	..	,, 250,000
1020	,,	2971	..	,, 500,000
405	,,	653	..	,, 750,00с
195	,,	230	..	,, 100,00с
681	,,	322	..	over 1,000,000

15053 million £ of which 10,500 million £ is held by 392,256 persons.

Thus we get two-thirds of the wealth held by just under 400,000 people, and the top one-third by 36,000 people. I think it is difficult to derive much *reliable* information as to whether the tendency is for individual fortunes to become increasingly great, that is for the proportion of wealth held by a fixed percentage of the whole population to become greater. The statistics have to be looked at over a considerable period, and they are affected by legal changes. The rates of mortality for the different age groups change slowly and affect the "multiplier," so that it is difficult to establish a statistical proof of a kind sufficiently rigid for so important an assertion.

One must remember that the rates of taxation now on the high incomes for death duties and income tax and super tax are so great that they are all the time exercising a profound modifying influence upon distribution of wealth.

How are the Different Factors of Production Rewarded ?

Let us look briefly at what we know as to the way our national income is distributed in rewarding the different factors of production. Dr. Bowley made a recent examination following upon the two assertions, viz., the statement by Mr. and Mrs. Sidney Webb, that the manual working class obtained for their need only one-third of the produce of each year's work, and Sir Hugh Bell's opinion that 75 per cent. of the *total sale value* of commodities produced went to pay the persons engaged in producing them. You will notice the two assertions are not quite the same thing. Many of the factors vital in Dr. Bowley's examination were figures provided by my own research, made quite independently of this question, and, indeed, he had for the most part to use proportions and details drawn for other purposes, but now combined and analysed for this particular enquiry. I have been over every item of the calculations carefully, and can find no flaw in them, with only one or two points of opinion on which I should have had a slightly different view, these being immaterial in the main result.

We reach the following division of the net output of manufacturing industries, covered by the Census in 1907 :—

	Million £.	Percentages.	
Wages	344	58⎤	
Salaries under £160 ..	24	4⎬	68
Salaries over £160 ..	36	6⎦	
Rents, Royalties, Interest and Profits	188	...	32
	592		100

We can obtain Sir Hugh Bell's 75 per cent. only if we count £40,000,000 of the profits, etc., as payments to employers for their share of production, which would be a not unreasonable method, for a sum comparable with this would pay their salaries if their businesses were turned into private companies, and they were employed as managers. Dealing with the possibility of a transfer from the salaries over £160 to the other classes, Dr. Bowley says : " It is very unlikely that the administrative and clerical staff is redundant in profit-making industries, and that the numbers could be diminished without loss to the output. If we suppose that the excess of every salary over £160 was transferred to wages, these would be raised only 5 per cent., and if only the higher salaries were attacked the average increase of wages would be negligible."

In the case of railways for 1911, which have hardly a total "product," 48 per cent. of the net receipts went to workers, and for coal mines, wages and salaries got 78 per cent. Dr. Bowley said : " In the whole group of industries for which we have adequate information, taken all together, excluding railways, it is found that 58 per cent. of the net product (after all other expenses and depreciation are met) goes to the manual workers, 4 per cent. in small salaries, 6 per cent. in salaries over £160 ; in all 68 per cent. goes to those employed. 32 per cent. is left for royalties, rents, interests and profits, advertisement, etc., and this is reduced to 23 per cent. if we count out royalties (as not being the result of the efforts of the employed) and allow 4 per cent. for the necessary repayment of our interest on capital invested. How far this 23 per cent. or £133,000,000, together with a relatively small sum (probably well under £10,000,000) for the salaries of managers of companies, is an excessive or unnecessary remuneration for the organisation of industry employing 6,000,000 wage-earners and £1,200,000,000 capital and producing

£340,000,000 wages, is a question that may properly be debated ; it is this sum that formed the only possible source of increased earnings in this group with industries conducted as before the war and production at its then level. In fact, while in some industries a considerable advance may have been practicable, in the majority no such increase as would make possible the standards of living now urgently desired, and promised in the election addresses of all the political parties, could have been obtained without wrecking the industry, whether by stopping the source of further investment or closing down firms whose profits were low. This statement in its general terms cannot, it is thought, be reasonably denied by anyone who has studied the facts."

Distribution of Rewards since the War.

As regards the post-war period, he said : " There is, at any rate, no proof that, reckoned at the prices of 1913, the national output when peace has been established, will be greater than before the war, even if there is no slackening of effort." Indications rather are that it is a trifle less at the present time. Dr. Bowley concludes by saying : " This analysis has failed in part of its purpose, if it has not shown that the problem of securing the wages, which people rather optimistically believe to be immediately and permanently possible, is, to a great extent, independent of the question of national or individual ownership, unless it is seriously believed that production would increase greatly if the State were sole employer. The wealth of the country, however divided, was insufficient before the war for a general high standard ; there is nothing as yet to show that it will be greater in the future. Hence the most important task—more important immediately than the improvement of the division of the product—incumbent on employers and workmen alike, is to increase the national product, and that without sacrificing leisure and the amenities of life." The period of the war, including the year 1919, presents great difficulties in any attempt to arrive at similar results. I may say, however, that for the year 1919 my own observation over a considerable range of accounts and business is that out of the total sum going in wages, salaries, rent and profits, some 60 per cent. went in wages, 20 per cent. in salaries of all amounts, and not quite 20 per cent. remained for profits (subject to Income Tax), rents, royalties and interest, and I, therefore, incline to the view that the last item, at any rate, until the repeal of the Excess Profits Duty, has lost some ground since the Census of Production results of 1907.*

* These results are substantially repeated for 1920.

CHAPTER IV

THE LIMITS OF TAXABLE CAPACITY

It will readily be realised that the three
previous subjects with which we have dealt,
viz., the amount of the National Capital, the
National Income, and the way in which they
are distributed, are essential preliminaries to
any consideration of taxable capacity. Apart
altogether from the question of figures and
amounts, there has been no public exploration
of the figures involved in measuring such
capacity, or, at any rate, it has been so spas-
modic and fragmentary as to be of little value.
It is only possible on this occasion for the
matter to be dealt with in its broadest aspect,
and I propose to consider rather the principles
involved than any mass of figures. Then,
when we have agreed upon the factors to be
taken into account, we can each attach to them
the arithmetical significance we prefer in our
estimates of present conditions, or our forecasts
for the future. In any case, I recommend you
to externalise your thought on the subject in the

manner I have previously illustrated, *i.e.*, by thinking of the question, as far as possible, as one of national production in a great " heap " to which we can all contribute, and from which we have to draw our subsistence. Only by taking these objective views can we prevent ourselves getting suffocated by words and figures.

General Ideas.

The idea of taxable capacity, or a limit to it, is one that has arisen quite recently in connection with :

(1) Government policy for the repayment of debt and other current expenditure, with the large budgets it entails, and

(2) the extent to which Germany can be made to pay for the war.

The term, was, however, used a great deal 25 years ago in discussing the alleged over-taxation of Ireland.

The taxable capacity of Ireland, as compared with England, and the relative amounts they were contributing to the Exchequer were then exceedingly live topics, and the Royal Commission on Financial Relations considered them at great length.

Some idea of the development there has been during this time in ideas relating to taxation can be obtained by reading the discussions which then took place. I referred to it in the Newmarch lectures last year in the following terms :—

Conflict with other Jurisdictions.

The great dilemma before State administration throughout the world at this time, in various forms goes right down to fundamental principles. It may be described as the conflict between " situs " and " ownership " as the basis of liability to taxation, or, to take the terms now becoming familiar, between " Origin " and " Residence."*

Twenty-five years ago when the taxable capacity of Ireland was being investigated and vigorously discussed, this difficulty ran throughout the matter, but was never really laid bare.† What is the taxable capacity of a country ? Is it what the residents in that country can afford to pay, or is it what the income produced in that country can justify ? Suppose that all the property in Ireland belonged to Englishmen resident in England, and all the property in England to Irishmen resident in Ireland, would the taxable capacity of Ireland be greater or less than that of England ? Are we considering the taxable capacity of a *people* or not ? We are back to the old contention that

* 1920 Comm. Evidence, 9573, etc. (S) ; Appendix, " Report of Sub-Committee on Double Taxation, p. 171.
† *British Incomes and Property*, pp. 367-9 (S).

taxes are paid by persons and not things. If you want to see how deep-rooted is the instinct to tax on two principles, imagine the feeling of an Irish Government imposing a separate Income Tax. Would they refrain from taxing a property in Sligo merely because the income from it went abroad ? One imagines that they would feel it was specially chargeable. But suppose that a millionaire settles down in Sligo who draws all his income from England, would they decide to exempt him ? Certainly not. It is very difficult for States to make up their minds which principle to adopt, and most of them end in taxing under both principles, hence the great problem of double taxation, which exists not merely as between this country and the Dominions,* but also as between the large and the small jurisdiction wherever federal government is found, and where co-equal juris-dictions exist within one economic sphere.

The United Kingdom was first in the field, and taxed on the principles of residence, origin, control, and every other pretext it could invent, on the Donnybrook Fair principle, " see a head, hit it." Now that the Dominions have heavy taxes of their own, we are faced with the problem of principle. Some of the Dominions charge on both principles of origin and residence, but others confine themselves to income arising

---

* On the whole subject *vide* 1920 Comm. Evidence and Report.

within their borders. France has been quite modest in her new Income Tax and has not charged income arising out of France.

Basis and Definition.

Elaborate attempts were made by the Commission to examine the relative power of the two countries by various tests, and also their *consuming* power. In the same way it is possible to deal with the total productive capacity of Germany, and to allege that such and such a proportion of it represents surplus that could be spared. It must be clear to you, however, that in so far as produce goes out to people beyond the state in question, it goes out to them for proper commercial consideration given, and these are not the people whom we desire to tax. They may be Italian or Dutch investors in German securities or property—they are not in fact the State itself. It is what is left to the *inhabitants*, together with what they derive from *outside* their borders—in short, the aggregate income of its inhabitants—that is the ultimate test. Who could think of ignoring Britain's investments abroad when determining her capacity? But, however useful a statement of aggregate production may be in *getting to* the answer to this sum, it is not in itself the answer. Everything depends upon the number of inhabitants, and it is obvious that 1,000 millions aggregate for a population of one million gives a taxable capacity quite different from what it would be if the population were 5 millions. We come back, therefore, to the question of aggregate income less the aggregate subsistence level as the first approach to the subject. So, therefore, the amount of Germany's resources is not so much the question, as the number of people who can divide them, and I ought to add also that a very material factor is the way in which the wealth is distributed. There will be a different taxable capacity if all the incomes are on one level or of an average amount, than if there is a steep graduation in distribution. If there are ten thousand persons at a level of £100 subsistence, and one person with a million £, there would be a larger taxable capacity than if the same aggregate of 2 millions were equally divided amongst 10,001 persons. This fact follows from the law of diminishing utility, upon which progressive taxation is based.

The Relativity of Taxable Capacity.

This question of taxable capacity is necessarily relative—relative not merely to our production, but also to how much we desire to save, and how little we are prepared to consume. If we put the saving at nothing, and are prepared to live on the barest subsistence, it is obvious we can stand a bigger

budget than if we consider our pre-war position
a privileged one to which we have a right before
we can be regarded as " affording " anything
for taxes.

Taxable capacity is measured by the difference
between two quantities—the total quantity of
production, and the total quantity of consumption. It is seen quite clearly that if the
latter is diminished the taxable fund increases,
and so attention is fixed upon this function,
and it is asked : " What is the smallest sum
upon which we can lead a reasonable existence ? " A large number are seen to live
perforce at a certain level, and it is postulated
that the remainder could also live at that level
quite as well. Multiply the number of people
by this level and so get the national subsistence
level. Deduct this from the number you first
thought of (that is, the national production)
and, hey presto ! you have the taxable capacity !
This is rather the attitude of some towards the
question of the proper degree of progression in
taxation. It leaves them cold if you refer to
the fact that a certain wealthy employer has
to pay away half of his income in income tax
and super-tax—£20,000 reduced to £10,000.
They say : " Don't talk to us of what we take,
see what he's got left. Most poor devils have
to be content on a mere fraction of it." As
Mr. Philip Snowden frequently says in effect in
his books : " *I always look at what we leave*

him." But taxation is not merely a stationary or static problem, the cutting up of an existing cake—it is a moving and dynamic problem. We have to ask not only how little we can leave him with, but also, how much reduction will he stand before he slackens in work and abstinence? How long will he come up smiling to be taxed in this way?

The Effect of High Taxation on Production and Saving.

Thus it is little use thinking of the consumption level only—we have to keep our eye on the production side too, and watch the effects of our action there. It may well be that as the consumption level is reduced by taxation, some temperaments will be tenacious of the old standard of comfort, and work *harder* than before to maintain the consumption level ; in this case a tax will make total production greater than before. Thus, a day teacher, finding his £350 reduced to £320 by taxation, may not want to break up his existing scale of expenditure, and he will give up some evening leisure and take evening classes to make it good. Taxation here creates its own fund of added utilities. But if the taxes are made very heavy, he will observe that the £50 he might have received for extra work is only £30 net, and he will not then be incited to effort. Similarly the desire to save may be quite discouraged by the low net yield after bearing a tax, and no attempt to save is then made. Then capital is less and production does not grow as it might—he may even dissipate the savings already made. Progressive taxation tends not merely to equalise incomes *after* they are made—it also tends to sterilise ability and ambition. For example, £400 a year for a special medical appointment may be very attractive to a medical man with £1,000 a year. Another man earning £3,000 a year through extra hard work and ability may be only just tempted to take it—the marginal utility of money is less to him, but the community is best served by his taking it, as he is the better man. Now, introduce progressive taxation. The £1,000 man gets, say, £900 a year, and the appointment is worth £350 to him ; the £3,000 man gets £2,000 net, and the appointment, on taxation, is worth only £200. He exclaims : " Not worth while for the effort ! " and the less able man gets it. Thus " marginal utility " operates twice over and in the same direction.

Successive Limits to Productive Taxation.

Now let us go back to production. If we make a reduction on the consumption level equal to 100 points by taxation, and so diminish willingness that production falls 20 points, we have reduced the taxable *quantum* by £20 and have reached one kind of limit of taxable capacity, though we may be still far from the physical subsistence level. For to secure the required revenue of 100 we have to impose a higher rate next time. We have reached the point of psychological reaction, which is far more important than the actual subsistence level. But there is another kind of limit—the point at which the revenue shows an actual diminution on an increase in rates of tax. Note the difference. Suppose the total income is 1,000 millions, and we draw out 2s. in the £ or 100 millions, and leave 900 millions. Now let the rate be 4s., diminishing incentive so that the total gross income is 850 millions—our revenue, at 4s., is 170 millions. We have reduced the consumption level remaining from 900 to 680, *i.e.*, by more than the total revenue, but we still have an absolute increase in revenue from 100 to 170. Now, let us increase the tax to 5s., the gross income drops, say, to 600 million £, and the tax is 150 millions. We have now not only a drop in the total production through the tax, but also an *absolute* drop in the revenue, and we have passed a second limit of taxable capacity.

The Pre-War " Standard of Living " Fetish.

In applying these ideas, most of us tacitly assume a kind of pre-war level of comfort and

I

subsistence, and regard a serious encroachment thereon as beyond our limit. But in the totally different problem of what Germany can afford to pay, we think mainly of her standard of production as fixed, and how low we can fix the subsistence level to give a maximum fund on which to draw. But she has her psychological limit too, and only actual slavery and individual taskmasters can get production from her people if no *part* of the increased production can revert to the producers, and if they can never rise over subsistence levels for many years.

I propose to put for your consideration the several reasons why the limit of taxable capacity is not an absolute or fixed figure :—

(1) It depends upon what the taxation is to be used for.

(2) It depends upon the spirit and national psychology of the people taxed, which may be influenced by patriotism or sentiment.

(3) It depends partly on the way the taxation is raised, both as to the methods adopted and the rate at which the increase is laid on.

(4) It depends on the distribution of wealth.

(5) Its rate of increase is greater than the rate of increase in wealth, and it shrinks more rapidly than the wealth diminishes.

The Application of Revenue.

The first point is probably the most important. There is undoubtedly a different measure of taxable capacity according to how the proceeds of the taxation are applied. It is impossible to say, without reference to this application, that a certain figure represents the limit of capacity. Thus we may apply taxation (1) to the reduction of debt within the country, (2) to the payment of interest on debt within the country, (3) to the payment of interest to people out of the country and (4) to the repayment of debt out of the country. Or we may apply it to investments which add to the productive powers of the country in other ways, in varying degree, such as capital extensions on post offices, telephones, and labour exchanges. We may apply it also to expenditure, which is practically unproductive, although in the last resort it may be necessary from a national point of view. As, however, we are dealing with the question of whether we deplete the total quantity of goods available for consumption below the necessary level, we must count expenditure on military and naval objects as being in a class by itself for unproductiveness.

Application to Internal Debt Interest.

First, it might well be that £500,000,000 would be the maximum that could be obtained if it were applied under the third head, payment of foreign interest, but it would not necessarily be the maximum applied under the other heads. Let us suppose that the nation's productive capacity is measured by a sum of £1,200,000,000, and the State has then contracted a War Loan on which it has to pay an interest of £300,000,000. This interest itself becomes taxable income in the hands of the recipients, so that the total taxable income now is £1,500,000,000, and, ignoring any other public necessities, the State has to raise £300,000,000 on this, which it would do by an income tax at 4s. in the £. Now the recipients of the interest pay £60,000,000 tax on their own £300,000,000, leaving £240,000,000 to be raised out of the original £1,200,000,000 of productive capacity. The net effect is that the producers get £240,000,000 less to enjoy out of their £1,200,000,000. But the £240,000,000 is not annihilated, in so far as the producers are themselves recipients of interest for past services and abstinence. The goods taken away from them in taxation by the State are returned to them. There is a shift over from the producers as taxpayers to themselves as receivers of interest of £240,000,000 out of £1,200,000,000. The net consumption of goods for the whole people is the same for their enjoyment and efficiency. Of course, it does not come back to them in exactly the same proportions, but it is quite in

a different case from what it would be if the
goods had been thrown into the sea. It is
only a charge upon the total national " heap "
in so far as there may be a few idlers, who
would otherwise have had to be putting on to
the " heap " in order to have their title to live
out of it, or, at any rate, to work harder, and
who are now kept in idleness by drawing out
of the " heap." But, certainly the bulk of the
subtraction from the heap goes back to the
producers in different proportions according to
their past efforts and service.

Now, suppose that the interest charge is
doubled, and becomes 600 million £. The effect
would be to give £1,200,000,000 plus
£600,000,000=£1,800,000,000 of taxable income,
at a rate of 6s. 8d. in the £, so that the
£1,200,000,000 would be reduced by the
£400,000,000 which gets shifted round. You
will see that the problem is not one of abstraction from production so much as the redistribution of proceeds, which is far less severe on
taxable capacity than abstraction. It falls,
however, heavily on a new producer who has
neither had War Loan himself, nor inherited it,
and such a tax is a deterrent to new effort.
Its immediate effect is small, but its dynamic
effect may be great. Therefore, this limit to
taxable capacity is not so much a limit to its
static capacity, but a dynamic limit to its future
producing power.

Application to External Uses, or Non-productive Uses.

Next, let us take expenditure on a foreign debt, or, say, military expenditure. The latter keeps men away from helping to increase production and the size of the " heap." They would otherwise have put on the heap as much as they drew off. Now they put nothing on, and the sum abstracted is something which either reduces general consumption, enjoyment and possible efficiency, or else it reduces the saving power for the future, in its net effect.

Application to Debt Repayment at Home.

We pass now to taxation for repayment of debt, and here I must ask you on this occasion, to omit the effects of deflation upon production. This taxation is a transfer of saving power. The State takes money away from B. which B. might otherwise have put into his business, or invested in a company. The State then proceeds to redeem the debt held by A. Then A. finds himself with new money to invest, and he puts it either into B.'s business or into the company that B. had his eye upon. This transfer of saving power may even *increase* saving if the producers are induced to keep their consumption lower than it might have been, and also, of course, if the recipients, when the debt is paid off, do not spend the capital as though it were income. The latter is a very rare event, and usually drastic taxation for the repayment of debt, at any rate speaking statically in the year in which it is done, increases the total saved capital of the country. Of course, if it is so heavy as to depress future effort, it has the dynamic effect of reducing production. You will see that there is not necessarily any net loss or real reservation out of the year's product for consumption. Obviously the whole saved fund might be taken in debt redemption if there were absolutely fluid conditions of transfer. When we are considering, therefore, whether the voluntary savings fund of the nation is kept intact after taking away the taxes, we can deduct from that savings fund the greater part of the amount which is being provided by taxes for debt redemption.

At this point, lest you should think I am beating the air with a discussion of barren principles, let us refer to a statement which has been the practical foundation of much that has been said on this question recently.

In a speech by Mr. McKenna at the Annual Dinner of the National Union of Manufacturers on June 14th, 1920, he made the following observations according to the newspaper report : " They would not expect him to give an exact calculation of our maximum taxable capacity. He could do no more than lay before them certain figures which might act as guide posts in the enquiry. In the year 1913-14 the Government expenditure amounted to about 200 millions, and the estimated savings of the community amounted to about 400 millions. Thus in that year the total national income exceeded the national expenditure, other than the expenditure by the Government, by 600 millions. The surplus of production over consumption would also be the same, but, measured in money, it would amount to a very different figure. The pre-war value of the £ sterling was about $2\frac{1}{3}$ times as great as its present value, and the surplus of 600 millions in 1914 would mean a surplus of 1,400 millions to-day. Thus, on the same basis of individual consumption, and on the same basis of production as in 1913-14 the total surplus we could possibly have to spend on government would be 1,400 millions, leaving nothing whatever for further accumulation of capital for the development of our trade and manufactures.

" Grave Over-Taxation."

" He did not think he was over-stating the case when he placed our present output at 80 per cent. of the output in 1913-14. (Cries of " Too high.") For his part, he believed that an

examination would show that a Budget of
1,000 millions was as much as the nation could
possibly carry at the present time, and that
even this figure would not leave a sufficient
margin for the increase of capital necessary for
the recuperation and development of industry.

" On the present basis of taxation the revenue
this year was estimated at 1,116 millions.
Some of the taxes, however, were not productive
for the whole year. In a full year the revenue
was estimated at 1,238 millions. The figures
he gave did not include anything for the sale
of commodities, but were the figures of ordinary
revenue. If it were true, as he believed, that
the nation could not afford to pay in taxation
more than 1,000 millions, the conclusion to
which he was driven was that we were being
gravely overtaxed." (Cheers.) Now, doubtless,
Mr. McKenna was fully alive to the considerations I have been urging, but it would
be quite unfair to expect, in an after-dinner
statement, on a hot evening in June, àny
exact review of all the issues involved. Others
have seized upon his general conclusion that
1,000 millions was a definitely computed limit,
and this has gained currency as a kind of axiom
in a way that he would not have desired. Six
weeks later, for example, the " Statist " improved upon his analysis by adding " The
taxation burden would not be less than 1,200
millions, leaving only a small margin of 200

millions, or less than one half of the pre-war amount to provide for depreciation in industrial capital, the continuation of new industrial enterprises, and the performance of various functions necessary to the economic vitality of the nation. With the increase in money values this 200 millions would have had the purchasing power of 85 millions before the war, thus making the total available for industrial purposes merely one-fifth of the pre-war amount."

So it is seen that a responsible organ adopts this method of approach, and in a recent criticism arrives at this conclusion.

Let us now set out this development of Mr. McKenna's line of argument, together with the points I have suggested :—

First Statement.

Pre-War Budget	200	millions.
„ Savings	400	„
Surplus of production over consumption	600	„
Present level of $2\frac{1}{3}$ times this would be	1400	„
Taxation burden is	1200	„

Leaves a balance of ... 200 millions to provide for savings and depreciation in industrial capital and new enterprises. This has a purchasing power of 85 millions before the War, and so equals one-fifth of pre-war savings.

If production has slackened the situation is even worse.

As revised.

Upon the principles I have set out :—

Surplus, as above		600	millions.
Now equals		1400	,,
Taxation (gross) ...	1200		
Take off the debt interest that is shifted round, and not consumed	350		
	——		
Effective taxation		850	,,
		—	
Leaves a fund of		550	,, towards savings
But some 200 millions are already provided out of taxes, which can be used for repayment of debt making in all for savings		750	millions.

Now the amount wanted is 400 millions multiplied by $2\frac{1}{3} = 933$, We have found 750 millions towards this, or four-fifths of the pre-war savings power, instead of one-fifth, as shown by the "Statist's" development of Mr. McKenna's views, always provided production is maintained.

The Level of Hardship.

The second main point that I wish to make is that taxable capacity will be different according to the level at which we define a real hardship to begin. Now the point at which men become grumblers and slackers, or the extent to which their efforts respond rapidly to limits in reward, are national characteristics, and one cannot assess them statistically. As I have indicated in the last lecture, the standard of life is by no means an absolute thing—it is relative to the age in which we live, and both poverty and riches are relative to the average standard of things existing. Moreover, it is not absolute, for you see that different civilised nations can have different levels. At the same time, I think there is little doubt that what we in England were thinking of as a reasonable standard, or a living wage for workmen of average ability, was a higher thing than the same idea in Germany, or in France, but probably not so high as in the United States prior to the War. Further, the point at which reaction sets in of a serious character, is not one that we can exactly determine, but neither can we afford to neglect it. It is conceivable that a strong civic sense, or a national call for patriotic effort, might afford a new standard of self-denial.

Now the level to which a country might reduce itself if we were exacting indemnities or the repayment of loans, would be unconsciously self-determined, but we might regard it as not sufficiently drastic, and by bringing pressure to bear, such as military occupation, or financial supervision, we might force it to something lower, getting the same production from the people. The difference would represent something that by pressure we had secured, but it would cost us money to do this, and we have to ask whether this would pay for itself, and the game be worth the candle.

Methods of Taxation.

Then the third point I should like to make is that the limit of taxable capacity may also fluctuate to some extent, according to the different ways in which taxation is raised. There are limits to the amount that can be got along one broad line, and here one comes up against the question of psychology very strong ly While we may, for convenience, reduce all the different kinds of taxes to one common denominator of a tax on income, the fact remains that the hardship created by imposing it as such a single tax on income, would be felt to a greater extent than if the poor tax payer is hit in different ways, under different guises, partly through indirect taxes and partly by death duties yielding an exactly similar amount. So when one tax is settled at a level at which people are beginning to feel it acutely, it pays not to add to that tax, but to try another kind, and it is here that the value of postponed taxation, like death duties, which come between the living and the dead, may be most clearly exhibited.

By a judicious mixture of methods one can get a larger sum out of the community (with a given amount of " pain ") than by following any one special line. The field of death duties offers possibilities at the present moment greater than additions to the already high direct taxation.

The mind and aspirations of man are very limited in their outlook in point of time. Beyond a man's own wife and dependents, perhaps, for 30 or 40 years ahead, he does not bother to look. If he did trouble, then he would object to spending money on leasehold property that is going to pass out of the possession of his descendants. If he did trouble, then reversions would have a greater value at a distance of time equal to 40 years than they actually have now, when their worth practically fades away.

But, to the State there is no such limit of life and thought. It can afford to take the longer view, and between these two there is scope for the State insuring itself a revenue by processes which will not appeal to the taxpayer as confiscation. I will not pursue this point beyond a general statement that taxable capacity is, to some extent, modifiable by relation to the system of taxes adopted.

You will realise, of course, that taxation by death duties gives greater taxable capacity in a stationary sense, and no destruction of capital whatever is necessary—there may be a mere transference. The only thing we have to worry about is its dynamic effect upon saving and enterprise. Of course, the capital levy, if it could really be guaranteed against repetition, would shift round the existing ownership of capital and remove debt, and might have no dynamic depressing effects upon the future.

Another important point is that, if you are going to depress the standard of living, and increase taxable capacity, you can get down to a much lower stage by doing it gradually, than by attempting it all at once. Nothing can be more obvious than this when you consider the way in which, in the year 1910, we were deploring the appalling weight of taxes and the absolutely suicidal policy of adding 3d. to the income tax, and encroaching on our reserves of war taxation. You have only to read the hysterics and homerics of those days to realise that education and compulsion will do a great deal. Just so, a certain dose of a drug will kill if taken right away, whereas by starting off with a small quantity one can ultimately work up to a much greater amount than this fatal dose, through the effects of "tolerance" by the human body, without fatal results.

The Effect of Extending Taxable Capacity.

As we have been thinking of this matter from the point of view of a surplus of production over consumption, we will continue that line of thought further. When people have to economise they can cut down laces and frills, concerts and pictures, before such necessaries as bread, meat, clothing, shelter. Hence, as there is forcibly extracted from the national heap the surplus for state needs, the residue for consumption tends to contain a greater *proportionate* amount of essential goods, and a small proportion of luxury services. Thus the heavy taxation of the rich means that butlers, chauffeurs, and valets would be discharged to go into the production of primary necessities, etc. It means also that the smaller surplus money to be spent by the masses on pure pleasure would mean fewer cinema actors, professional footballers, and the like. The character of the " heap " would begin to change with, of course, much economic upheaval. Similarly the very disproportionate amount of our total labour engaged in distributing and marketing, with all its duplication and over-lapping, may be forced by heavy taxation to adjust itself into an economic organisation with a more economical transmission of power and with prevention of waste. In most of our thoughts about our own taxable limit, we tacitly assume for ourselves both an unaltered organisation of *existing* production and a pre-war standard of comfort and savings, but for the Germans a narrower level of subsistence. While this may be strictly just, we have to ask whether it may not lead to our failing to search for, and to find, means of increasing our net production per head, such means including the problem of distribution. May not the German nation, reduced to a bare subsistence, provided its spirit is not entirely gone, gradually searching after a modicum of luxury, learn to economise in effort, find short cuts, reduce oncost, and so produce its subsistence with diminishing total effort ? If the German becomes servile, and actually content with a bare existence, we may not get enough production for indemnities to be paid. If he works hard to repay, we may find stern necessity has put him ultimately ahead of us in organisation and method. If the advantage that we have derived by having our own surplus of production over consumption amplified by his contribution, has been consumed and not saved in capital goods for production, we shall start level at the end of the reparation period as to the *mass* of productive power, but he will have all the advantages of the improved methods forced by necessity. If we do *not* consume the indemnity, but save the appropriated surplus, we shall match that advantage by an alternative advantage of greater invested producing power. It will be almost a contest between the advantage of the objective aids to production we shall have received and saved, against the subjective habits and organisation for the economic good the German will have developed.

The Present Capacity in Theory.

Some concrete notion as to my idea of our present taxable capacity may be expected. I do not think it quite fair to start on the assumption that we must consume exactly what we did before the War, and have no larger surplus than we then had. I am going to assume that we might have saved 100 millions more, and that we could have spared 50 millions more in taxes, without having a really unhappy and down-trodden existence, or without dislocating the economic organisation too much. Then the surplus of production over consumption would have been (in millions) :—

	£ Millions.		
Taxation	200+	50	250
Savings	400+	100	500
			750

This, out of 2,250 million £, would have represented practically 33 per cent. of the total income.

At twice the level of values this surplus is represented at 1,500 millions. But we shall not collapse if only *half* the pre-war rate of saving is assumed, and if the balance goes to pure taxation. Let us say the saving is even now £500 millions. I will presume that three-fifths of this can be done *via* debt redemption. We then have :—

£ *Millions*.

Aggregate surplus (present values)	...	...	1,500
Less :			
Individual savings	...	200	
Savings, *via* debt redemption	...	300	
		——	500
Available for taxation as surplus	...	...	1,000

Let the normal taxation eat up the actual
surplus   1,000
Add taxation which does not absorb surplus :
Interest charge changing hands 350, deducting a proportion for the due effect on
production by individuals, say 100   250
Add : Debt redemption, money changing
hands   300

Nominal Budget £1,550

Assumptions.

(a) Pre-war production attained.

(b) Pre-war consumption curtailed 10 per cent.

(c) Pre-war rate of savings halved.

(d) No losses brought about by rapidly falling prices.

Conclusion.

We could just stand a budget of 1,250 million £, plus 300 million £ debt redemption = 1,550 million £ in all.*

This is equal to an Expenditure Budget of 900 million £ without interest on debt or redemption, to include all increases in the local rates.

* NOTE.—It should be noted that although this conclusion has been quoted as if it were applicable to present conditions, the arithmetical assumptions on which it rests do not represent present conditions. The result must be modified by the extent to which actual conditions differ from those postulated.

Practical Limits to the Theory*.

These figures are, so to speak, ideal, especially because they stand against a hypothetical set of figures as to national production. It will be difficult surely, to suggest that, even when the strike is over, our present production is more than 80 per cent. or 85 per cent. of the pre-war figure. This factor, after all, is vital to any calculation, and an assumption must be made as to the actual present facts (May, 1921). If pre-war *income* (not *quite* the same thing) was £2,200 millions, and personal consumption £1,600 millions, the present representation of these figures in pre-war terms might be put at 1,760 to 1,870 million £ and 1,440 million £ respectively, the consumption being cut down 10 per cent. This gives a margin of 320 to 430 million £. If our present price level is 125 per cent. above pre-war figures, then for 1921–2 this becomes a margin of 720 to 960 million £, as the aggregate surplus. Allowing a mere 50 millions from this for *ordinary* savings, and treating 100 millions (per the Budget speech) as being applied to debt, we get a surplus for taxation of 570 million £ to 810 million £. Now, out of the total Interest charge I will take 200 million £ as not being a real abstraction

* The passages following were added in remarks before the *Political Economy Club* after the Budget of 1921.

from surplus, and the debt redemption of £100,000,000 I treat also as an addition to the savings, making total savings a paltry 150 million £, or less than a sixth of the pre-war amount. We thus get the trial Budget, on the Chancellor's present lines to a limit of 870 million £, to £1,110 million £ (according to whether production is 80 or 85 per cent. of pre-war amounts), while the actual Budget is 964 million £ (excluding non-tax revenue) plus 80 millions increase in rates, or a total of 1,044 million £. You will see, therefore, that it is a very tight fit, and if production is down below 80 per cent. on pre-war volumes, it is no fit at all. At the best it means a very small accretion to capital, and a standard of living reduced below the pre-war level in real value.

Moreover, if values are declining, the Budget is affected to a more than proportionate extent, because the capacity to meet the assessments based on higher values is so seriously impaired.

My conclusion is, therefore, that if production can be maintained and prices do not decline, the Budget is just within our powers for 1921-2, but that 1922-3 will tell a different tale unless things rapidly improve in production. Even 1921 depends upon matters going no worse than they are at present. In any case, taxation must be severely felt, and not very much addition to National Wealth is possible.

CHAPTER V.

THE EFFECT OF CHANGING PRICE LEVELS UPON PROFITS AND WAGES.

THERE are three aspects from which we may consider this subject. There is, first, what is said about it in general economic teaching ; then the light thrown upon it by statistical research ; and, thirdly, what we may expect as to the future from general economic reasoning.

The Effect of Changes in Currency upon Prices.

What has in the past been a purely general and " long-distance " problem has, of course, now become a short period and very acute one, and it may well be that if we reason from the one class of phenomena to the other we may go seriously astray. It is, however, due to past experience that we should question it narrowly and see how far it supports reasonings from first principles, and generalisation from individual cases.

It is impossible to get far upon this subject unless we try to form some idea of the way changes in price level get into action, so to speak, or, rather, how differences in purchasing power translate themselves into differences in price level. It is an extraordinarily difficult thing to discern in action, because it is so silent and impalpable, being the result of the thoughts of so many people, which act in what we call a " market," that it is hard to put one's finger upon the change at any point.

The old type of change in price level, following upon the change in the volume of the gold stream, was not so difficult to discern if examined quite broadly for its effects. We can well imagine that the increasing abundance of the gold supply—or the relative ease with which, owing to new processes, it made a full return upon the capital and labour expended in extracting it—had an immediate influence upon the exchange of goods surrounding the mines. A real disparity between the capital and efforts required to obtain gold, and those necessary to produce other forms of commodities in the neighbourhood, could not long stand unchallenged, and equilibrium has come about naturally, partly because the miners and mineowners have had a larger effective purchasing power, and, therefore, a " stiffer " demand, and also because the suppliers of their grocery and clothing were obviously not going to be content with a less command over purchasing power in reward for their efforts than could be obtained in the mines. Viewed in the abstract, and with fairly obvious examples in practice, there is, of course, a flow of labour and capital from one class of industry into the other until equilibrium is obtained. Hence we get a general rise of prices in the commodities coming into contact with the " gold stream " at its source.

Now, looking at past instances, if all the gold remained in the vicinity of the mines, prices would have gone very high indeed ; but, of course, the high prices attracted imports from abroad, and the gold went out to pay for them. The new supply of gold in the exporting markets began to take its effect there too, particularly if, as in modern times, the gold supported a large superstructure of proportionate credit. An example of how this came about may be found in the history of prices, and particularly the effect of the stream of precious metals into Europe in the early sixteenth century. It did not have the effect of simultaneously raising prices in all parts of Europe, but prices were raised first where the gold and silver stream came into contact with civilisation, *i.e.*, the importing and navigating countries, and the higher prices gradually found their way into the more remote corners of the European continent until the effect was very considerable indeed. Jevons was able to predict with considerable accuracy the effect upon Europe of a serious fall in the value of gold, even to the precedence that the increasing prices would take in regard to effect upon raw materials, foodstuffs, animals, and so on.

Differences in the Effects of Increased Credits.

Our modern problem is one of the manufacture of credit, like the discovery of a gold mine in each of our back gardens, and as this starts more or less in the *middle* of the whole economic machine, it is much more difficult to say exactly where it originates, or to trace its effects. Supposing that each bank manager were to decide that in the past he had been much too cautious as regards the amount of assets which he kept in reserve against his loans to traders— that is to say, in the proportion of the deposits made with him which he ought to keep back ready to meet the calls of depositors.   Then, of course, people applying for advances on goods and securities for expanding their trade, would find it much easier to get them, and the effective purchasing power through this credit would be suddenly greatly enlarged, though it would be more or less hidden in the breast of each merchant and manufacturer.

At the same time you will, of course, presume that there has been no increase in the quantity of goods to be purchased, and in that subtle way in which a market price is constituted, the buyers in competition put up the prices, the sellers feel the trend, and we find the wholesale prices of imports and raw materials rising. The third sort of inflation that we have to cope with to-day arises without any alteration in the actual ratio of advances made by the Bankers. I will not stay to explain it here, but when the Government borrows on " ways and means " advances, the Banks ultimately get a new basis of assets by their deposits with the Bank of England, and without actually altering the apparent ratios of ordinary Bank reserves, industry may be enabled to exert a larger nominal purchasing power. Here it is as if we multiplied the reserves by a factor, and thus gave ourselves the power, while still preserving the old ratios intact, to give larger loans. The use of currency notes is, of course, consequential upon this, or what Professor Nicholson calls " pulverising " the new credit into little lumps for general and retail use, for wages and the like.

Some have thought that credit and money were identical in influence upon prices. Credit is indeed purchasing power, and helps to raise prices, but credit has not to the same extent the power of liquidation. As Professor Seligman says :—" Credit, though it exerts by no means the same amount of influence on prices that money does, exerts the same *kind* of influence. The reason that it does not exert the same amount of influence is that a portion of its ideal efficacy as a substitute for money is lost," through the necessity of immobilising the reserve ; "the extent of the reserve is a measure of the incompleteness of the substitution, and therefore, of the degree to which credit fails to equal money in affecting price." Of course, you can get an increase of price without any change in this level of purchasing power by a general rarity of commodities, and this was one of the causes of high prices during the War. One cannot account for an increase in the price of an article *merely* because it is scarce—that is, measuring its price in other articles. For example, a pound of butter may be worth three pounds of sugar, and the total quantities of each may be reduced by 50 per cent., and yet this relation of three to one may still hold, so that the mere rarity of commodities *as a whole* does not increase the price, except the price in money, which has not been made equally rare. It is most important to bear in mind this distinction. Inflation comes about whenever we get multiplication of purchasing power without the corresponding multiplication of goods. This does not originate, generally speaking, in the hands of consumers, but in the hands of traders. Therefore, the wholesale prices usually rise first, and more than the retail prices, and in a similar way they fall first. A real distinction exists, but cannot be pursued here, between expansion which works off its own effects by a permanent increase of goods, and other classes of credit multiplication. The fluctuations of the wholesale prices are more violent, and trading profits consequently rise before wages or professional incomes ; they also tend to fall before wages or professional incomes. The effect of a rise in prices gives the maker of profits an even greater profit than he could otherwise secure, because his expenses, lagging behind, bear a smaller relation to his total receipts. We should expect to find, *primâ facie*, therefore, that profits, being an economic margin, increase to a much greater extent than the immediate increase of prices, until all the expenses, including the cost of purchasing stock and paying wages, have increased in proportion. Then at that stage the increase in the actual profit made (not the rate of profit on turnover) would tend to be proportionate to the increase in prices. We know this to be a fact from many separate instances, and also that the converse holds good upon a fall. But what do we know upon the matter for the country as a whole ?

*Statistical Research upon the Actual Effect
A Changing Price Level.*

Speaking from the point of view of statistics, we are on very difficult ground. On the question

of the effect of changing prices on profits, we
have singularly little real investigation, and I
am the more diffident and hesitant about putting forward what there is, because it rests, so
far as I know, upon my own researches, and,
therefore, I have not the advantage of an
independent check by other workers to enable
me to avoid the personal factor, which is just
as dangerous in statistics, as it is in experimental
physical science.*

We have various partial measures of trade
changes existing over a long period of years,
but it is difficult to get any aggregation of
profit made up on a sufficiently uniform plan
to correspond. If we select a given group of
businesses of which we know the profits, it is
almost impossible to get uniform details of
their total trade ; moreover, the group is
probably too small for us to be confident that
individual idiosyncrasies will have cancelled
each other, and it is not easy to keep a complete
series for a sufficient number of years to secure
that the cycles of trade shall be fully represented. In short, there are very formidable
difficulties in the way of making a proper
comparison between profits and trade statistics.

I have set out to examine the figures, and
then to ask what would be the increases if the
natural growth of population were taken into

* Several passages here are reproduced from the *Journal* of the
Royal Statistical Society, July, 1918.

account, and how far was the increase in profits
due to a real increase in output of commodities,
as distinct from an increase due to higher prices
for the old quantity of goods.

If a given measure of trade has risen say,
from £100 to £120, and we rejoice in a rise of
20 per cent., it may be that either 120 units
have been sold instead of 100, at a regular
price of £1, or that 100 units have been
sold at a price of £1 4s. each instead of £1, or
the result may be a combination of both changed
quantity and changed price ; it may even be
that one factor has actually *diminished*, but
that its effect is more than offset by the increase
in the other.   What is the actual or probable
change in profit that accompanies such a
change of 20 per cent., according to the cause
of the change ?   Will a like change accompany
a second, or third ensuing rise of 20 per cent ?
Will the relations found to exist for increases
hold also for decreases, or what difference may
we expect ?

Now, I am not going to put you through the
lengthy disquisition that I gave the Royal
Statistical Society, because I there had to
discuss material rather minutely, and also
methods of getting fluctuations into an index
number, clear of the normal growth of population.   I applied, I believe, for the first time
in this country, the method of representing
the normal growth by a straight line, which is

called the linear secular trend, and then I measured the fluctuations or deviations from that line. The line itself may not actually join the figures at the two ends of the series ; indeed, it may actually touch none of them, but it represents the best straight line " fit " for the points all taken together. (*Vide* figure 2).

When one is dealing with a long time-series, there is absolutely no other satisfactory way. I then compared the fluctuations of one series showing profits with another showing prices, and another showing volumes, and tried to find how far the fluctuations were connected, both as to the time they occurred and the amount of the fluctuations, by scientific methods.

Fluctuations in Coal-Mining Profits.

Using the Pearson co-efficient of correlation, I came to the following general results for coal mining : Apart from the *degree* of deviation, the *correspondence* of deviation in the case of tonnage compared with profits is close—profits have generally increased more than the average where tonnage has increased more than the average, and decreased similarly. But the effect is, of course, mixed up with increases and decreases in price. In the comparison of price-changes with profit-changes the correspondence is found by all tests to be very close indeed. Where profits are reckoned as including the almost stationary item of royalties, then, for a change in price represented by one point, profits changed something like 3 points. A rise in prices had rather less effect in raising profits than a fall in prices had in diminishing them, and where the rise or fall was large the change in profits tended to be greater in proportion than it was for a small rise or fall. Where a year of rising profits was followed by another rise (or a year of fall followed by another fall), the succeeding year tended to show a diminished factor, *i.e.*, the effect of the price change in altering profits was not so great This I assume to be due to the rapidity with which wages followed prices. When I excluded royalties from my series of profits, I came to the conclusion that price was four times as powerful as output in causing fluctuations in profits. But profits and prices in coal-mining were not always indicative of changes in the same direction in other industries. Thus I found a very high negative correlation between the profits of railways and the price of coal, so that improved profits in collieries meant reduced profits in railways. I found the same sort of negative correlation between gas profits and coal prices.

Fluctuations in Other Trades.

When I examined Merchants' profits I found that the fluctuations in total profits were almost

COAL MINING, 1888–1915.

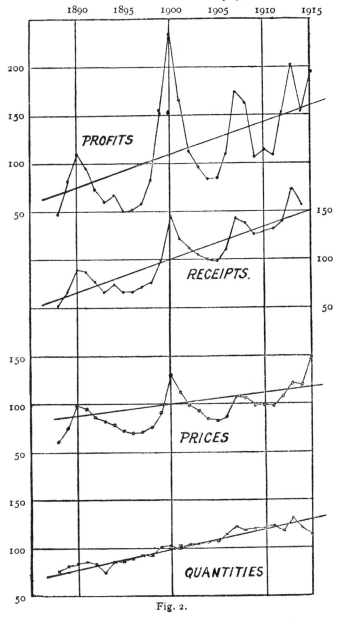

Fig. 2.

entirely those due to the amount of sales, and the results were unaffected by price changes.

In the case of cotton spinning, the changes were remarkably violent, the deviation of the price from the trend of prices was very extreme, averaging 14.4 per cent. on the average price, but the deviation of profits from the average profit was 154 per cent., or nearly 11 times as great.

Then I made an elaborate calculation to get the profits for the country as a whole, presenting them in one series for 35 years, and I should like any of you interested in the subject to look closely at the graphs which I drew from 1880 to 1914, as they are by far the best way of inspecting these results. My conclusions were as follows :—

The fluctuation in profits has generally been rather less in *magnitude or range* than the fluctuation in statistics of " turnover," such as banking or foreign trade statistics, which reflect both quantities and prices, and it may be taken roughly at two-thirds to three-fourths of such short period changes in trade returns.

The influence of a change in price level on profits *as a whole* is far less than is frequently supposed by those who base their views upon observations of the striking effect of price changes in particular industries.

In times of rising prices, increases in profits have been made over and above the amount

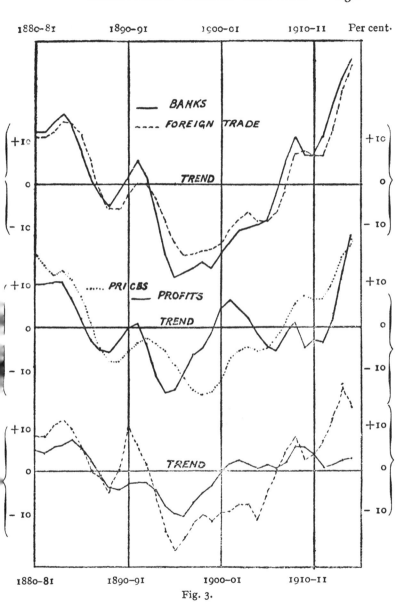

Fig. 3.

that would arise upon the increased output that such prices induce, but the additional profit is not usually much greater in proportion than the rise in price, if the period taken is not less than a year. There is no evidence as to the effect of such changes measured over shorter periods than a year.

Although the increased quantities evoked by increased prices have followed quickly enough to keep profits within such limits, the check has not been permanent, and continually renewed stimulus by the raising of the price level has resulted in increases of profits much greater than could have followed the ordinary increase in output (due to increasing population) at a constant price level. Similarly the drop in prices from 1880 to 1895 kept profits down considerably below what would have resulted from the *actual* output at a constant price level, and in itself was instrumental in depressing that output.

Those who would like to look at the matter on much broader lines, may be content with the following totals of Assessed Profits under Schedule D. (from " British Incomes and Property.")

A Broad Comparison of Three Periods in the 43 Years Prior to the War.

From 1872 and 1873 the Index number dropped from 110 down to about 86 for 1879-80, or, say, 24 points in ten years. It then dropped

from 86 to about 62 in 1896, or 24 points in
15 years. It then rose from 62 to 85 by 1914,
or 23 points in 18 years. Now, the comparable
series of profits, including, of course, the
changes due to the growth of industry and
population, went from 235 to 284 in a corresponding period of years, or 49 points in 9 years,
say, 5.44 per annum. It then went from 284
by extremely slow stages to 349 in 1894, or an
increase of 65 points, or 4.33 points per annum.
From 1895 it rose from 366 to 687, an increase
of 321 in 20 years, or, say, 16 per annum. The
rise over the whole period averages just under
10 per annum.

Now, if we set these results side by side, we
get the following :—

Period.	Annual Price Change.	Annual Profits Change.	Difference between the annual charge and the increment of 10 per annum over 42 years.
1872–3 to 79-80	—2.4	+5.44	—4.56
1879–80 ,, 1895–6	—1.6	+4.33	—5.67.
1894–5 ,, 1914	+1.3	+16.0	+6.0.

This, perhaps, will be some indication of the
way in which the long slow dragging prices
through the 'eighties to the middle 'nineties
kept down the rate of profits, and the wonderful
spurt that followed the increased gold supplies,
when the cyanide process got fully into
operation in the middle 'nineties. It was about
1885-1886 that a Royal Commission was

appointed to consider " Depression in Trade,"
and it is not uninteresting to read, even in these
days, the evidence and findings of that Committee.

Changes in the Average Income of the Income Tax Payer.

Now I should like you to look at an interesting
comparison that I have made in another way.
We have already considered the general belief
that colossal incomes have increased under
modern capitalism, out of proportion to the
increase in the population, but I have shown
you that the number of persons enjoying an
income of modest dimensions, has also increased
so greatly that the slope of distribution has not
been greatly altered.   These effects combined
would serve to account for the fact that the
average income of all the persons *with over* £160
per annum has not greatly increased, but the
number of persons with such incomes has
increased in a much greater ratio than the
population, viz., an increase in tax payers of
320 per cent., against a population increase of
59 per cent. We are concerned, however,
rather with the fluctuating fortunes of this
" average " taxpayer than with his position in
the whole population.   When he gets his
nominal income, what is its real value, or
purchasing power ?   I have divided the average

by the Sauerbeck " Statist " index number of
wholesale prices (for the three years immediately
preceding), and also by Mr. G. H. Wood's
retail index number (continued by the Board of
Trade retail index number) for the actual year
itself, and taken the mean of the results, in
order to get figures which shall be as firmly
based as possible and free from the accidents
of individual methods or series. (Each index
number has been taken on the series in
Mr. Joseph Kitchin's charts as equated to
100 at the year 1900). The " real value " of
the average assessed income is given in Col. 5
of this Table, and it will be seen that its course
has been much freer from wide fluctuation than
the nominal average and the maximum range
of £200 has been lowered to £100. It would
appear that the widespread depression in trade
that had followed the decline in price levels
after 1872, had by 1881 affected the average
profit to a greater adverse extent than was
made good to the *spender* in the reduced prices
themselves, but that by 1894 business had
become more settled at the lower levels of
prices (before the 1896 turning point in gold
production began the new upward trend) and
the spender had the full benefit of the cheapness
of commodities. Since then, as a spender of
income he has lost the apparent advantage
that he has obtained as a maker of income.
I made a correction of the earlier figures to

allow for deficiencies in tax administration, &c.
By giving an increase of 10 per cent. on the
figures 50 years ago, and diminishing the
addition by ·2 per cent. per annum, the results
can be seen broadly in Figure 4. These results
are, I think, notable. The dotted line C.
represents the real value of the true average

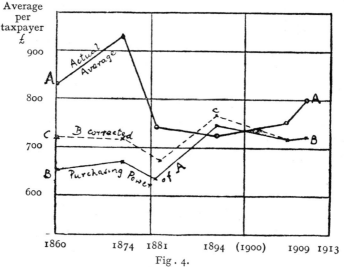

Fig. 4.

assessable income in each year observed. Apart
from the depression in 1881 and the appreciation
in 1894, the line is almost level, and with regard
to the latter I would only remark that the
income tax law has throughout been such that
the fluctuations in the agricultural interests are
hardly represented at all, and if the true income
of farmers had been given its effect upon the
general average, the depression in that industry

1.	2.	3.	4.	5.	6.
Year.	Taxable income (millions).	Number of taxpayers (incomes over £160) (thousands).	Average taxable income per taxpayer. Col. 2 — Col. 3.	Purchasing power of average income. Col. 4 × index number of prices.	Purchasing Power of *real* taxable income. Col. 5 corrected for improvement in income-tax administration
	£		£	£	£
1860—61	232.9	280.4	830	656	721
1874—75	440.3	473.8	927	670	718
1881—82	468.7	632.2	741	635	672
1894—95	551.4	761.7	723	746	759
1909—10	831.0	1100	755	719	719
1913—14	951.0	1190	799	723	723

in 1894 was so great that it would have reduced the prominence of the average for that period.

This result should not be in any way confused with the statements in Chapter III. about the general upward movement of *all* incomes during the century. For it would be possible for all incomes so to move upwards, that while the bottom one is resting upon the exemption limit, the average of all would be the same as the average of *all over* £160, when only *half* the people were above the level. It just depends upon the spread of incomes above that figure, and the above indicates merely another aspect of fluctuation in money values.

Changes in Wages from 1880 *to* 1914.

The question of changes in wages is one which is in difficulty almost equal to that of profits, though the difficulties are very different in kind. We have, however, the advantage that we are not wholly dependent upon an exact aggregation, but can work upon index numbers of changes, without any serious liability to error. There is, of course, a difference between the change in the average per wage-earner, and the change in the rates that we can discern in separate well defined industries.

There has been an increase in the general average through the movement from the lower paid occupations to the better paid, such as come about through the new entrants into industry tending to move towards the industries that are better paid.

Dr. Bowley, who is our greatest living authority on wages, says that the increase in the average earnings of the manual working class as a body, is greater than that found in separate industries.

The main source of our information is the index number published in the abstract of Labour Statistics, which is obtained from the changes of time rates in several industries, building, engineering, and agriculture, together with piece wages, textiles, and mining. It is defective in several ways, because total earnings rarely change in proportion to changing piece rates, and of course, does not tell us anything about the differences in numbers in the different industries, and it covers only a limited field of industry.

Before the Royal Statistical Society, Mr. Wood made some important investigations, in which he weighted the average of the different sets of wages, and also allowed for the more rapid growth of the occupations that are better paid.

Then Dr. Bowley has also given index numbers, and from all these three we can form a pretty close idea as to the movement of wages over a long period. You can find this set out year by year from 1880 in Dr. Bowley's essay

on the " Change in the Distribution of Income."
The average wage per earner has increased in
the 33 years to the War at almost exactly the
same rate as the average of all incomes, and we
get the following table : :—

Year.	Average of Wage-incomes.	Wholesale prices. (Sauerbeck).	Cost of living. (Mr. G. H. Wood's method.)	Real Wages.
	expressed as percentages of their levels in 1880.			
Col. 1.	Col. 3.	Col. 4.	Col. 5.	Col. 6.
1880	100	100	100	100
Average 1881–5	101	91	96	105
,, 1886–90	104	80	89	117
,, 1891–5	110	76	88	125
,, 1896–1900	115	74	87	132
,, 1901–5	121	80	91	133
,, 1906–10	126	87	94	134
1911	128	91	96	133
1912	132	97	100	132
1913	134	97	100	134

The rate of growth of wages has not been
uniform. Sometimes wages gained a little on
other classes of incomes for a time, then lost
again. If the 33 years are divided up to 1898,
the first 18 years wages increased 13 per cent.
and the second 15 years 18 to 19 per cent.
This apparent greater annual growth in the
second period when set against the movement of

the price level, gives a somewhat different impression.

If you look at Sauerbeck's index number it will be seen that there is a fall amounting altogether to 25 per cent. in the first period, and then a rise bringing it back to the original level. As you know, however, the Sauerbeck number relates to wholesale prices, and this, of course, is only a secondary measure of retail prices, and, therefore, only a third-rate measure of the cost of living, which includes rent and other direct payments.

Dr. Bowley says : " The figures are sufficient to show that the average real incomes increased much more than 16 per cent. in the first period, and much less than 20 per cent. (if, indeed, they increased at all) in the second period. Mr. Wood's researches enable us, however, to get a little closer to the question of the cost of living, which considerably modifies the rise and fall shown by the more violent fluctuations of wholesale prices."

He goes on : " It is doubtful whether any amount of research would improve on Mr. Wood's approximation, although some of the details are open to criticism. There is no official series of retail prices, even of food, which covers the period on a uniform system." If these cost of living figures are applied to the index of wage incomes, we get, curiously enough, the same total increase in the 33 years, but we establish the fact that it had all been achieved by the middle 'nineties, and that there had been hardly any improvement or variation in real wages since 1898 up to the War.

Dr. Bowley comments "that there were slight ups and downs and variations in regularity of employment, but the general movement was so small that the precision of the estimates was not sufficient to detect it.

" It was not uncommonly alleged immediately before the War. that real wages had fallen. Although I do not accept the truth of this statement as being demonstrable on the evidence, if the average of all wages is in question, yet it is undoubtedly true if we ignore the part of the progress due to the numerical increase of the better paid occupations."

He concludes : " That the majority of men below military age at the beginning of the War, began their adult working life after the date of lowest prices, 1896, and throughout their experience as householders they found prices rising against them, and having chosen their occupation, have not benefited by that part of the increase in average wages which is due to the shifting of the rising generation to better paid work.   Such men were naturally not impressed by demonstrations by statisticians, including myself, that they were better off than their fathers had been."

The Effect of a Drop in Prices upon Profits.

When we come to consider the important question of the effect upon industry of a considerable drop in prices, of course, nearly everything depends upon the readiness with which money wages accommodate themselves to the changing level.   Even if we assume that they respond readily, there is still a great fear of substantial losses through having to cut prices upon accumulated stocks.   The price tends steadily towards the price appropriate to the costs of the most recent contribution to the fund, thus reducing the value of all the less recent as and when sold.

Before the Commission on Financial Risks, it was commonly alleged that just as traders made an extra profit equal to the rise in prices on stocks in hand, and the Government took a large slice of it in Excess Profits Duty, so they would make an *equal* loss on the fall in prices, and the Government should, therefore, bear it.   Against this it was argued that by careful buying there need be no loss upon the decline but only a rather reduced profit.   Let us glance at the broad elements of this matter, ignoring wages changes, which we will assume to move in sympathy with reasonable rapidity, or to be incorporated in the price of stock bought.

Let stock=Sales over 6 mo

1st Pe

Stock at beginning	...	1,000 at £1	=
Purchases	... ...	1,000 at £1	=

£

2nd Pe

Stock at beginning	...	1,000 at £1	=
Purchases	... ...	1,000 at £1 10s.	=

£

i.e., a rise of £500 on stock and

3rd Pe

Stock at beginning	...	1,000 at £1 10s.	=
Purchases	... ...	1,000 at £1 10s.	=

£

i.e., same percentage on turno

4th Pe

Stock at beginning	...	1,000 at £1 10s.	=
Purchases	... ...	1,000 at £1	=

Loss, £400. £2

i.e., the drop in price on w

10% on purchases.

ꓛNARY PRICE.

					£
...	...	...	1,000 at £1 2s.	=	1,100
at end	...	...	1,000 at £1 (cost)	=	1,000

Profit, £100.   £2,100

OF 50% IN PRICES.

...	...	...	1,000 at £1 13s.	=	1,650
at end	...	...	1,000 at £1 10s. (cost)		1,500

Profit, £650.   £3,150

ᴐn in addition to normal profit.

ONARY PRICES AT THE HIGHER LEVEL.

...	...	...	1,000 at £1 13s.	=	1,650
at end	...	...	1,000 at £1 10s. (cost)		1,500

Profit, £150.   £3,150

ᴏfit rises 50% like prices.

IN PRICES TO FIRST LEVEL.

...	...	...	1,000 at £1 2s.	=	1,100
at end	...	...	1,000 at £1	=	1,000

£2,100

less the ordinary profit.

M

Broadly speaking, it may be said that the losses to be incurred by industry upon a rapid drop in prices, are a function of the total stock carried at any moment in all stages, from the first producer to the retail shopkeeper, in relation to the turnover in the period over which the change takes place. As many people are rather hazy as to the actual effects of a change in prices upon stock in hand, I give below some hypothetical examples which, of course, are simplified to such an extent that they are not true to the facts of life, but only bring out the particular point we have in mind to examine. I have assumed that, on the price level being doubled, all features, including the profit, will also be doubled, *i.e.*, that the same rate of profit as a percentage of turnover is maintained. If we think of profit along its economic definition, as being a margin accruing to the more favourably placed businesses compared with those only just able to maintain production at a given price, then there is no reason to suppose that upon a magnification of all the monetary elements of the situation, they should not all be similarly affected.

From the tables it will be seen that if R. equals the rate of profit, T. the turnover, P_1 and P_2 the two levels of prices, and S. the stock, then Profit $= \frac{1}{R} T.P_2 + S. (P_2 - P_1)$. From this, if it is assumed that in a certain period turnover or output is three times stock in hand at any moment, we can get the relation between $P_2 - P_1$, or the drop in price to the rate of profit on turnover and the stock. If the amount of stock in industry before the war was 1,200 million £, and that at the present time is 2,800 million £, the return to a half-way level would mean a reversion of the stock of this quantity to 2,000 million £, i.e., there would be a loss of 800 million £ on the stock*. Unless this is to bring disaster in its train, it must come about so gradually as to be absorbed by a reduction and not a total cancellation of ordinary profits. Thus, if the pre-war turnover was 4,000 million £, and a corresponding figure is now 8,000 million £, and if the old profits were 400 million £ at 10 per cent., and the present profits 800 million £ at the same rate, a reduction of the rate of profit by one-fifth, i.e., to 8 per cent., would be a provision of 160 million £ per annum towards this loss. It will be seen, therefore, that the effect of such a change in price level might be, so to speak, absorbed by a moderate reduction of the average rate of profit in some 7 or 8 years. If the total quantity of business done, however, increases considerably, this does not necessarily mean that there need be so great a reduction in the absolute amount of profit accruing to industry, provided that the increased business

---

* These figures are quite hypothetical, as the true ones are unknown, but the relations hold good for purposes of illustration.

is done not upon a larger stock, but by a more rapid circulation or turnover.

It is to be feared, however, that we have started upon such a rapid reduction that the economic ship of industry will not soon come on to an even keel, and the gradual reduction, which is the essence of the matter if the translation from one level of price to another is to be achieved without disaster, is already hopelessly beyond attainment.

CHAPTER VI

General Principles.

In considering the subject of the effect of changing price levels upon the burden of public debt and taxation, I intend again rather to consider only the principles involved, with a few illustrative figures, than to make an elaborate calculation to arrive at some fixed result. The whole application of these principles lies in the future with its unknown movement of prices, industry, and population, and, therefore, any attempts at final or accurate results would be a waste of energy and quite devoid of value.

Involved in these considerations are all the matters which we have been discussing hitherto, such as the Amount and Distribution of National Capital and Income, the Limit of Taxable Capacity and the Effect of Prices upon Profits. The subject before us is one that cannot be approached until after these others have been examined and clarified.

Evils of a Shifting Standard.

The social disadvantages of a standard or measure of deferred payments, which fluctuates as violently as our standard has lately done in its real value, must be clear to us all when we look at the present welter of wage increases and bonuses, and the necessity for rapid and drastic alterations in what seemed to be such stable and fixed conditions as railway fares, doctors' fees, and penny postage. Nowhere is this more obvious, and nowhere does it give rise to greater apprehension, than in connection with the burden of debt. For when prices are high, the nation incurs a debt which has to be repaid later according to a standard of value which may obtain in the future, and the debt also bears interest on that fluctuating standard, so that the real value or human effort represented by the terms arranged, may change violently. Either the nation is burdened beyond justification or the lenders are penalised. There is no escape from the dilemma.

The Real Character of the Burden.

You will remember that in considering the minimum of national subsistence, we put back into the national "heap" that part of it which, as interest paid by ourselves, was taken out in the guise of taxation, and paid back to

ourselves in the guise of interest, and considered that it was not a final abstraction from
the heap as it would certainly have been if it
had been taxes spent on war material. Individuals are not receiving it back in the proportions they pay it, it is true, but there are
said to be 17 million holders of State Debt,
and I thought that it might be dealt with by
cross entries in our personal books to a very
considerable extent, and thus also fail to affect
our national minimum of subsistence adversely,
to the extent of, perhaps, 200 millions, out
of the whole 350 million £. The balance
was allowed to be a real abstraction, but I was
careful to point out the *dynamic* effect of such
taxation on the production of future heaps,
particularly because increasing their size was
to be a very important element in remedying
our ills. A man may be unaffected in
his efforts, *so far as they at present exist*,
by the payment to, and receipts from
State interest, but every *new* effort at saving
and every *new* responsibility will also come
under taxation of a drastic kind, and makes
the reward far less attractive. It, therefore,
dulls the keenness of his appetite for improvement and also for abstinence to some extent.
Then, what is worse, there are continually
coming into the productive field numbers of men
who had no war savings and receive no interest.
Their new business enterprise or saving is

taxed to pay tribute for the past abstinence of others. The prizes of successful enterprise and risk-taking are seriously reduced, and the dead hand of past debt stretches out over the zeal of future generations. It is possible to exaggerate the importance of this, for rewards and returns are relative and not absolute. If a generation is born into certain conditions, and has known no better, it may acquiesce in these more readily than we think, and accept them as part of the natural order. But if taxes are too steeply graded upon the rewards of ordinary successful enterprise and originality, the nation as a whole may lose far more than it gains. It will be a bad day for the less efficient when they unduly paralyse the rewards of the more efficient, who, in benefiting themselves, also contribute an unknown but none the less real benefit to the whole nation.

The Changing True Weight of the Burden.

Suppose that the State has borrowed £100 from you in the sterling of the day, and undertakes to repay you in five years' time. It then proceeds to print £1 notes until prices are four times as high as they were ; so that you find, upon getting back your £100, that it is only worth to you a quarter of what it had previously been. You have been robbed, so to speak, of three-quarters of your rights.

Such a wilful action as this might well be stigmatized by the title "repudiation," just as much as a definite refusal to repay ; and there are some who suspect that this is what is actually happening in some countries in Europe to-day. If, however, the change in values is not brought about wilfully, people are less prone to give it such an ugly name, but regard it as " the fortune of war." When a nation avowedly sets out to cheat its creditors in this way, it is, of course, running the risk of ruining its whole economic organisation by inflation and all the ills to which that action leads. But what happens in the converse case ? The nation wishes to follow the difficult but praiseworthy path of gradual deflation, the elimination of paper money, and the return to a stable standard based upon the precious metals. All history and economic reasoning goes to show that this, if possible, is the proper thing to do. A standard based on the fluctuating and fortuitous total amount of credit is liable to be more open to abuse, but a definite policy of getting back to gold can be understood. Two great difficulties, however, face the nation that wishes to follow the path of virtue. First, as I showed last week, the declining price level means a damper on business optimism. Inflation is like a drug, and business men love to work under its influence ; they feel they are doing great things ; there is progress and prosperity everywhere, and if it can be kept within bounds there is no doubt that, like the rum ration, it enables them to do surprising deeds and to go " over the top." It needs some courage to follow year in and year out the definite path of deflation, just as it needs, perhaps, more skill than we always possess to keep it within reasonable bounds. The second difficulty is that the nation sees its fixed charges for interest and repayment of debt becoming a larger and larger proportion of its total income and resources. It borrowed from a man during the War what was equivalent to a pair of boots, and in ten years' time it finds it may have to pay back what is the equivalent of 2 pairs of boots.

This may be indeed no great hardship if the total production has so increased that two pairs of boots represent a smaller fraction of that total than one pair was at the time when the loan was made.

To revert to our figure of the national " heap." If the heap remains approximately the same in actual goods, but the money tokens by which it is shared are fewer, the receivers of debt interest and repayment are entitled to the same money tokens, and, therefore, a larger and larger share of the heap. Only by the heap being made substantially larger as the money value of individual items diminishes, can the actual proportion of it in physical objects which are transferred to these recipients, be prevented from increasing.

It is small wonder, then, that at the present moment we have a growing body of opinion that deflation is a wrong policy, and that we should try to keep prices somewhere about the present level. There are some who consider that we should not allow any material deflation until we have repaid a substantial part of the debt ; they say, with much force : " Let us pay back these lenders in the same kind of money that they lent us, for, if we do not, the burden will become intolerable." For example : a debt charge of 350 million £ a year, or, say, 270 million £ net, represents, out of a net national income of 3,500 million £ one-thirteenth part (say, 7½ per cent.) of the real products and services of the country. Now, when the money value of these services and products has been cut down to 2,700 million £, it represents one-tenth, or 10 per cent., and when that money value has got back to its pre-war figure, it represents more like one-seventh, or 12½ per cent. It would seem to be a desirable policy from this point of view alone, that we should not allow deflation to proceed faster than our redemption of debt, in order that the annual interest charge should not be an increasing proportion of the total real production, but should either be a constant proportion or a lessening proportion. Moreover, if we deflate too rapidly prices drop so quickly, and profits shrink so seriously in consequence, that our difficulty in raising sufficient taxation to make a substantial reduction of debt becomes greater. We are, therefore, other things being equal, more likely to be successful in making a substantial repayment and keeping the burden from becoming greater if we do not deflate too rapidly. Following this principle, by the time prices drop so that the national income is 2,700 million £, the debt charge ought to be a *net* figure of 208 millions only, which means that we should have to repay something like 1,200 to 1,500 million £ of debt while prices are dropping.

What does it really amount to when people say " we should not pay people back more than they have lent us ? " The money has not been lent to us with prices at their present level, and there is still room for considerable reduction before we reach a point when we consider giving them more than they have given us. At present if we repaid we should be giving them less.

A Measure of the Real Values lent in the War.

The following table shows the average index number, and, roughly, the amounts borrowed in each year :—

Year.		Index.		Million £ borrowed
1914	...	85	...	410
1915	...	108	...	1167
1916	...	136	...	1629
1917	...	175	...	1985
1918	...	192	...	1682
1919	...	256	...	323
				7196

There are 700 millions of pre-war debt, so this is sufficiently near, I think, for our purpose. Now, from this you can calculate the weighted average index number for the whole borrowing is 161, whereas the index number at the present moment (February, 1921) is over 200, showing that we have to drop 40 points before we can be said to be paying back at greater values than we borrowed*.

The first repayments of war savings certificates are now falling due, and as the index number in 1916 was 136, we appear to be innocently guilty of "repudiation" to the extent of some 6s. 6d. in the £.

The Burden of the Annual Charge.

Deflation makes a much greater difference to income than to capital if it has the effect of reducing the rate of interest. For this

* This position has virtually been reached. (December, 1921.)

reason it is much better to think of this problem in terms of the annual debt charge and annual redemption of debt, than of the total debt and the total national capital. The national capital does not come down by deflation as fast as the national income, because many sections of it increase in value, such, for example, as the values of ground rents, debenture and preference interest. Although the stream of profits becomes smaller, the rate of interest on deflation also comes down, and the multiplier or number of years' purchase goes up. Suppose the "stream" is £200 a year, with interest at 8 per cent., or 12½ years' purchase, there is a capital of £2,500 of which £500 debt would be one-fifth ; but when the "stream" has dwindled to £100, and the rate of interest is 5 per cent., or 20 years' purchase, there is a capital of £2,000. The income is half, but the capital is four-fifths, and the £500 debt represents one quarter of the whole. You will see how misleading it is to represent the burden of debt in terms of capital rather than in terms of interest.

Deflationary Effects of Repayment of Debt by Capital Levy.

The advocates of a capital levy put forward the points to which I have referred about the increase in value of money as a strong reason for repaying as much as possible at the present moment, and not burdening the future with a proportion of taxation increasing in relation to its total efforts. Now, of course, this big question raises many other considerations, such as the feasibility of the tax, its effect upon industry, the psychological influence in politics, but I think · we are bound to say that the repayment aspect of the matter is, perhaps, the strongest and most powerful feature in favour of this course being taken.

However, even the drastic redemption of debt brings about its own problem. Every repayment of debt represents a considerable force, making for deflation, in so far as debt is being used as collateral security and forms a basis of credit. You withdraw such basis and the credit supported thereon shrinks with deflationary effects. It is possible, therefore, that a large repayment by a capital levy might have two sudden effects ; first, the deflation would be so rapid as to dislocate business, and thus destroy the stream of productivity prematurely ; and, second, the immediate burden of the remainder of the debt might be greater both as to interest and principal than it would have been if deflation had taken place gradually. In so far as the advocates of the capital levy rely upon the plain question of the proportion which the charge bears to the national income, their ground seems to be perfectly sound. They would say that if productivity expands, but the aggregate money value of income is unaltered, the real payment which has to be made in interest on the debt will have grown in the same ratio as productivity. But productivity may not grow so fast as money values shrink. Professor Pigou made certain assumptions as follows :—Assumed income 3,000 million £, including the income of War Loan holders. Reduction in War debt will carry a reduction equivalent to interest saved :—

(1) If no levy, the revenue required is 800 million £ out of 3,000, or 27 per cent of national income.

(2) If half repaid, the revenue wante dis 560 million £ out of 2,800 million £, or 25 per cent.

(3) If all wiped off, the revenue wanted is 320 million £ out of 2,500 million £ or 12 per cent.

This ignores the effect of redemption upon prices (deflation), which would operate to increase the later percentages, and minimise the differences, if the rest of the Budget is assumed to be relatively constant.

Alternatives to Repayment by Capital Levy.

Those who do not like the prospects of an inflationary policy or of a capital levy, have to put forward their policy. Upon what do they rely ? First, they rely upon a general increase in the population, and therefore, of business, which so increase the total national income that, despite the increasing value of money, the burden will not become greater. Relying upon this alone, it is obvious that the commercial activity and output of the country must increase more rapidly than prices diminish, Let us look at what happened after the Napoleonic Wars :—

The Course of Events after the Napoleonic Wars.

After the Napoleonic wars the debt was some 850 million £, or about £52 per head of the population. At that date the national wealth was about £159 per head, so that the debt was one-third of the national wealth. In 1914 it was less than 5 per cent. of the national wealth. The fixed charge for the debt service in 1817 was about 8 per cent. of the national income, and in 1914 a trifle over one per cent. The price level went from 142 to 85. The growth in population, wealth and earning power made the debt of 1817, as years went on, an unimportant burden. Of course, there were additions during the period, of £73 millions for the Crimean War, and 281 million £ in the Boer War. When we are considering the recovery that was made, we must remember that the trade and commerce of this country in the early Victorian era had such a prominence as leading the world in the new order, with the revolution in transport and credit systems— really quite as important as the much vaunted industrial revolution, and much more far-reaching—that a wonderful spurt took place

N

which we can hardly expect to be repeated in the future. Past the " bloom of youth " in our coal and iron resources, we may well hope to plod along and make good progress, but we can hardly expect a sensational leap to new wealth and producing power. If the debt charge was 8 per cent. of the income in 1817, and it is now 10 per cent., is it reasonable to look for such a markedly rapid release by the mere spread of the burden over a wider population ?

In 1864, 47 years later, the national income had doubled, notwithstanding the drop in prices from the index of 142 to 100, and in 11 years more (1875) it had trebled with prices a little lower ; in 16 years later (1891) it had quadrupled with a price level of 72, or just half the 1817-18 figure. The same national debt charge that had stood at 8 per cent. of the income, if untouched, would have been 4 per cent. in 47 years, $2\frac{2}{3}$ per cent. in 58, and 2 per cent. in 1891.

But what happened to the debt during this time ? The funded debt was approximately :—

		Million £.
1817	...	880
1840	...	766
1842	...	773
1846	...	764
1848	...	774
1854	...	755

So it will be seen that during the long fall in prices from an index of 142 to one of 74, in 37 years, it was a very hard struggle with the capital debt, and not much was really *paid off* in the ordinary sense of the word. It was only the increasing wealth and population that made it more bearable.

Leroy Beaulieu put the burden of the debt at 9 per cent. of the income in 1815, 5½ per cent. in 1843, and 2½ per cent. in 1877. The following shows the approximate " true " charge per head* :—

Date.	Total Debt.	Per head.	Charge.	Per head.			Index No.	Index charge per head.
1817	850	50	32	£1	17	0	142	260
1833	789½	32.19	28	1	3	0	91	252
1842	841	31.9	28	1	2	0	91	242
1854	803	29.6	28	1	0	0	102	196
1857	836	29.15	28.8	1	0	0	105	191
1867	801	26.10	26.1	0	17	0	100	170
1886	742	20.9	23.7	0	13	0	68	191
1895	659	16.13	25.0	0	13	0	62	210
1903	798	19.4	27.2	0	13	0	70	186
1914	707	15.7	24.5	0	10	0	85	118
1920	8078	175.12	332.0	7	16	0	248	629

Mr. Fisk computes that six years of war added more debt than the preceding 226 years.

The magnitude of our total is, roughly, ten times that of the last century. Shall we then reduce our debt by only 450 millions in 37 years?

*The first four columns are taken from Mr. Harvey Fisk's ' English Public Finance," p. 166.

The charge for the debt was equally slow in
its change :—

1817	...	32 millions.	
1840	...	29½ ,,	
1844	...	30½ ,,	
1853	...	28 ,,	
1860	...	29 ,,	(nearly).
1870	...	27 ,,	
1880	...	28¾ ,,	
1885	...	29½ ,,	
1891	...	25 ,,	

It was one long struggle between two great
movements, viz., the increase of population
against falling prices, in which the former
slowly won the day.

Relief of Burden by Reduction of Interest.

So much, then, for the first hope of ameliora-
tion, repayment of debt.

The second thing upon which we have to
rely is conversion of debt. As most of you
know, an opportunity for reducing the burden
upon the nation arises whenever a debt falls
due for repayment. Suppose that we are
paying 5 per cent. on a £100 Bond falling due
in 1928, we can in that year, if the rate of
interest has, as we anticipate, become lower
owing to general deflation in prices, borrow the
£100 from other people at the new rate of
interest, say, 4 per cent., repay the loan and

go on thereafter with a debt charge reduced accordingly. Of course, in the case of the long-dated loans, the decline in the general rate of interest will throw them automatically above par, and unless we are prepared to make the loan-holder suffer, we are helpless. To buy his loan at above par in the market is as broad as it is long, because we have to borrow a larger sum than the original debt at the lower rate of interest. But relief in the current charge may be obtained by giving a larger nominal amount of debt (when falling due for repayment) in exchange for present relief in interest.

Now our total indebtedness is fairly well spread. We have falling due in the next 4 years (including our whole indebtedness to the States) some 1,687 million £, equal to about 422 millions per annum, or, without the United States, about 205 millions per annum. In the following five years there is about 1,907 millions coming due, then there is a stretch of some 10 years during which repayments are negligible. Then we have from 1942 to 1947 2,124 million £, and in 1960 409 million £. This seems to make up substantially the total indebtedness. But the floating debt, though a serious problem by reason of its size and the inflation which it tends to bring about, is the one which answers most readily to the reduction in money values, because if we want to repay it and have the power, we can do so at any

moment, and in so far as we want to continue
it we are able to do so at the reduced rate of
interest provided by the market. So far as
past history is of value in our present troubles,
it is interesting to note that during the 19th
century conversion gave very little re ief.

The yield of Consols. was	4%	in	1817.
,, ,,	3.4	,,	1833.
,, ,,	3.0	,,	1882.
,, ,,	2.8	,,	1889.
,, ,,	2.7	,,	1894.
,, ,,	2.4	,,	1897.
,, ,,	3.0	,,	1909.
,, ,,	3.3	,,	1914.
,, ,,	4.1	,,	1915.
,, ,,	5.2	,,	1916.
,, ,,	4.5	,,	1917.

The only refunding operation that made a
saving commensurate with the effort involved
was Goschen's in 1888 and 1889, when 565
million £ at 3 per cent. was refunded into 2¾
Consols., at a saving of £1,411,000 a year, and
the rate in accordance with the terms arranged
became 2½ per cent. after 1903. Gladstone's
effort in 1853 came at an unfavourable time,
and similarly the 1884 operation saved only
£46,756 on £22,362,000 of debt.

The numerous and complicated Sinking Fund
provisions for sections of our present debt make
it clear that a good part of the debt must disappear in the ordinary course.

Foreign Comparisons.

It is now of interest to make some comparison between our problem and others abroad.

The percentage of the total expenditure required for debt service is about 29 for the United Kingdom, against $15\frac{1}{2}$ in the United States, and $23\frac{1}{2}$ in France. The only ones who budget for an excess of revenue over expenditure are ourselves and Czecho-Slovakia. Japan is raising by taxation 78 per cent., the United States 89.7 per cent., and Germany $53\frac{1}{2}$ per cent. of the total expenditure.

The figures used by the Financial Conference in Brussels, based upon my calculations of national wealth and income per head,* gave the present Government Revenue per head as a percentage of national income per head as follows :—United States 9, United Kingdom 27, France 18, and Germany 12, Italy 13, and Japan 13. But the expenditure per head bore, of course, a different percentage to income per head :—U.S.A. 9, U.K. 22, France 40, Germany 23, Italy 30, Japan 17.

International statistics of debt are interesting when expressed as a ratio to current revenue : —France 10 years' purchase, Italy 7.5, Germany 7, U.K. $5\frac{1}{2}$, U.S.A. 4.2.

* " The Wealth and Income of the Chief Powers." The Brussels figures contain so many purely speculative elements that they must be used with the greatest caution, as merely indicating an *order* of magnitude and not actual facts.

The burden of debt per head as a percentage of average income is also important :—

United States ... 34 (22 if debt from abroad is excluded).
United Kingdom ... 151 (116 do.
France 180
Germany 86
Italy 95

A Hypothetical Prospect.

If we suppose that in 15 to 20 years we have received :—

1,000 million £ in repayment from the Dominions and Allies
1,000 ,, in indemnity
1,000 ,, by application of sinking funds,

we may then have a debt of less than 5,000 million £, representing, say, about 225 million £ per annum for debt service. Let us assume that re-borrowings on maturities for a debt of, say, 2,000 million £, have reduced the interest by 20 millions. The charge would then be 205 millions, and if the population has then increased at not less than its old rate of growth and is over 60 millions, we shall have a money burden of about £3 8s. per head, instead of £7 16s. per head. If prices have gone down by 50 per cent. of their increase over pre-war times, this will represent a real burden of something like £4 10s. per head. But a greatly increased production per head would do much to improve the relief. Such figures as these are not put forward as having in themselves any intrinsic probability, but only as some indication of the order of magnitude of the changes involved.

New Schemes of Finance.

I have no intention of going far into this field, which would demand a volume to itself. But the debt seems likely to be with us for so long, that there may be something in that very fact which gives room for principles that can find a proper application only in age-long conditions.

The State, unlike the individual, does not die—it can take the long view. It can, therefore, finance by methods which would be too far-reaching in the scope of time involved for individual businesses. It might even pay us to sell life annuities on terms more favourable than precise actuarial prices. With the capital sum debt would be immediately redeemed—the annuity payment would slightly exceed the old interest charge, but when it ceased, the debt and its interest would certainly be gone for good, whereas, in the ordinary course, it still remains to be paid off, even 40 years hence. It would cease to be profitable only if the difference between the annuity and the interest over the life period were more than a sinking fund payment for the whole loan period to provide the capital sum at the due date of payment of the loan.

Possibly what is known at the Rignano plan of death duty taxation might also be specially adapted to take advantage of the gap between the " time-horizon " of the individual and that of the State. The taxation of inheritance progressively as the inheritance becomes more removed from the original saver, would not penalise the individual worker—it might make him work the harder to know that nearly all he himself produces and saves will pass intact to his sons, whereas what he has inherited from his grandfather will be heavily taxed. After about 50 to 60 years very large sums would be passing to the State which could be applied to extinguish the debt. Thereafter, if one dare look forward so long and speculate as to the constitution of society at that date, the special principle of taxation could be modified or abolished and the rates of taxation at each successive inheritance relaxed.

*　　　*　　　*

In conclusion, I should like to state that, while I feel I have but imperfectly sketched some of the principles of the mensuration of wealth in its national aspects, I have been covering a field that has by no means been fully explored, and I should be failing in my duty if I did not make an appeal for workers in this field of statistical study. It is true that the pursuit of this kind of knowledge has little of the excitements of those branches of investigation which are attached to daily polemics, and the honours to be gained in it may be meagre and not of the most ostentatious kind, but work undertaken with the true scientific spirit is never really lost or unimportant, and in this sphere it may very quickly be its own reward. There is a growing need for data on these subjects, compiled without partisanship or bias,— free, so to speak, from its practical applications,— to which all those engaged in the toil of thought for the national betterment, may turn with gratitude.

INDEX.

INDEX. 195

CHIEF REFERENCES.

BOWLEY, PROF. A. L. : *Change in the Distribution of Income,* 1880-
1913.
——— *Division of the Product of Industry.*
CRAMMOND, EDGAR : *Royal Statistical Society Journal,* 1914.
FISK, HARVEY : *English Public Finance.*
INTERNATIONAL FINANCIAL CONFERENCE, Brussels, 1920. Report
IV. Public Finance.
STAMP, SIR JOSIAH : *British Incomes and Property.* 2nd edition,
1921.
——— *Trade Fluctuations and Profits. Royal Statistical
Society Journal,* 1918.
——— *Wealth and Income of the Chief Powers,* 1919.
——— *Fundamental Principles of Taxation,* 1921.
——— *Estimate of Capital Wealth of the United Kingdom
in Private Hands. Economic Journal,* 1918.
CENSUS OF PRODUCTION REPORT, 1907. Cd. 7320.
INLAND REVENUE, 63rd Report of the Commissioners of the, 1921.
Cmd. 1083.
INCOME TAX, Royal Commission on the, 1920. Appendix.
Cmd. 615.
INCREASE OF WEALTH (WAR), Select Committee on. Report and
Evidence. 1920. P.102.